Library of
Davidson College

THE *WISDOM* SYMPOSIUM

The *Wisdom* Symposium
AMS Studies in the Middle Ages, No. 11
ISSn 0270-6261

Other titles in this series:

1. Josiah C. Russell. *Twelfth Century Studies*. 1978.
2. Joachim Bumke. *The Concept of Knighthood in the Middle Ages*. 1982
3. Donald K. Fry. *Norse Sagas Translated into English: A Bibliography*. 1980.
4. Clifford Davidson, *et al.*, eds. *Drama in the Middle Ages: Comparative and Critical Essays*. 1982.
5. Clifford Davidson. *From Creation to Doom: The York Cycle of Mystery Plays*. 1984.
6. Edith Yenal. *Charles d'Orleans: A Bibliography of Primary and Secondary Sources*. 1984.
7. Joel T. Rosenthal. *Anglo-Saxon History: A Bibliography*. 1985.
8. Theodore John Rivers, trans. *Laws of the Salian and Ripuarian Franks*. 1986.
9. R. C. Famiglietti. *Royal Intrigue: Crisis at the Court of Charles VI, 1392–1420*. 1986.

THE *WISDOM* SYMPOSIUM

Papers from the Trinity College Medieval Festival

EDITED BY
Milla Cozart Riggio

AMS PRESS, INC.
NEW YORK

Library of Congress Cataloging-in-Publication Data

The Wisdon symposium

   (AMS studies in the Middle Ages, ISSN 0270-6261; no. 11)
   Includes index.
1. Wisdom (Morality play)—Congresses. 2. Moralities, English-History and criticism—Congresses. 3. Christian drama, English—History and criticism—Congresses. 4. Jesus Christ in fiction, drama, poetry, etc.—Congresses. I. Riggio, Milla Cozart. II. Series.
PR644.W58W57 1986   822'.2   85-48070
ISBN 0-404-61441-8

Copyright © AMS Press, Inc., 1986
All rights reserved.

Manufactured in the United States of America

AMS Press, Inc.
56 East 13th Street
New York, N.Y. 10003

Contents

	Preface	xi
I.	The Staging of *Wisdom* MILLA COZART RIGGIO	1
II.	"Blake and wyght, fowll and fayer": Stage Picture in *Wisdom* DAVID M. BEVINGTON	18
III.	The Play of *Wisdom* and the Abbey of St. Edmunds GAIL McMURRAY GIBSON	39
IV.	Is *Wisdom* a "Professional" Play? DONALD BAKER	67
V.	*Wisdom* and the Records: Is There a Moral? ALEXANDRA F. JOHNSTON	87
	Index	103

Illustrations

COLOR PLATES

1. Christ as "Eternal Wisdom," by Heinrich Suso
2. King Edward IV enthroned
3. King Edward IV, his queen and son, etc.
4. King Henry VI and his parliament at Bury St. Edmunds
5. Abbot Richard Hingham and St. Edmund
6. Trinity College Medieval Festival production
7. The Ghent Altarpiece, by Hubert and Jan van Eyck

BLACK AND WHITE ILLUSTRATIONS

(following p. 52)

Two views of the abbot's palace, by Edmund Prideaux

Monastery of Bury St. Edmunds before the Dissolution, by W. K. Hardy

Contributors

MILLA COZART RIGGIO
Trinity College
Hartford, Connecticut

DAVID M. BEVINGTON
The University of Chicago

GAIL McMURRAY GIBSON
Davidson College
Davidson, North Carolina

ALEXANDRA F. JOHNSTON
Principal, Victoria College
The University of Toronto

DONALD C. BAKER
Professor Emeritus
The University of Colorado at Boulder
now teaching at Wuhan University
Hubei, China

Preface

The decision to stage *Wisdom* at Trinity College in 1984 resulted mainly from a desire to rescue this morality play from the dramatic limbo to which critics and editors alike had consigned it. To show that *Wisdom* is a good play, to redefine its genre, and to set it in a plausible fifteenth century context: these were the aims of the Trinity Medieval Festival. As much a masque as a morality, *Wisdom* belongs among the stately, choreographed performances and exemplary antic entertainments that led to the later masque tradition. This at least was the hypothesis we tested in The Wisdom Symposium organized around our production of the play. As I describe it in the opening chapter of this book, that production recreated an aristocratic dimension of morality drama and conjectured a possible link between monastic politics and lavish entertainment. In essays written for the symposium, David Bevington, Gail Gibson, Donald Baker, and Alexandra Johnston unite in their claims of excellence for the play and in their common focus, though differing in their conclusions. More like chapters in an ongoing inquiry than separately conceived papers, these essays debate issues raised by the Trinity production. Bevington discusses the way *Wisdom* actualizes visual metaphor; Gibson links the play to the fifteenth century Abbey of Bury St. Edmunds, illustrating the frequency with which the monastery's abbot entertained royalty; Baker questions the notion that this is a learned play reserved for a pious, elite audience, arguing that *Wisdom* might instead have been presented by a small troupe of professional players; and Johnston offers an alternative explanation of the play's aristocratic staging.

Three of the essays have been revised for publication: David Bevington's "'Blake and wyght, fowll and fayer': Stage Picture in *Wisdom*" and Gail McMurray Gibson's "The Play of *Wisdom* and the Abbey of St. Edmund" appeared in *Comparative Drama* and are reprinted through the courtesy of editor Clifford Davidson; Milla Riggio's "The Staging of *Wisdom*" was published in *Research Opportunities in Renaissance Drama* and is reprinted by permission of editor David Bergeron. These essays, visibly toughened for print, now differ in style from the papers by Donald Baker and Alexandra Johnston, the oral quality of which we elected to preserve. We were met, as Donald Baker remarked, in celebration of the play, and we would like our readers to share some of the directness of exchange and casualness of tone that enhanced our debate.

I want to thank Borden Painter, Dean of the Trinity College Faculty, for Trinity's generous support of *The Wisdom Symposium*. The Connecticut Humanities Council endowed the symposium itself. Others to whom the Trinity production, the symposium, and this book owe their existence include John Alves, Martha Banks, David Ericson, Brian Rieger, John Woolley, and the devoted undergraduate cast of the play—Jeffrey Butler, Deborah Bliss, Jordan Bain,

WISDOM

Matthew Bradley, Ellery Brown, Joe Scorese, five "prudent virgins," and a dozen dancers as well as Nancy Katz, our stage manager. Matthew Moore, Sarah Ragland and other members of my Festival and Drama course helped to host the symposium. Joseph del Principe wrote the musical score, provided the musicians, and directed the music for *Wisdom*; Jill Beck choreographed the dances. My children, Anna and Tommy, added elegance and devilry to the play; my husband Tom kept us sane by laughing at us. But, most of all, we owe this event to Roger Shoemaker, whose direction of the play proved that *Wisdom* could for a moment almost seem, to steal a phrase from Lucifer, "gloryosest of ony creature þat euer was wrought."

Milla Cozart Riggio
Trinity College
Hartford, Connecticut
May, 1986

The Staging of *Wisdom*

MILLA C. RIGGIO

Recreating medieval drama for modern audiences is as much an act of explication as of entertainment; each detail of staging, costuming, and directing carries the weight of interpretive commentary. Thus, when we decided to stage *Wisdom* at Trinity College, the real challenge was not just to find resources sufficient to the technical demands of a complex play, but to explicate the dramatic text in a performance that dispelled the persistent notion that *Wisdom* is a dull Christian sermon made palatable by some timely, if irrelevant satire.[1] To provide as varied a perspective as possible, we staged Wisdom twice—once as a banquet masque on April 12-14, 1984 (in conjunction with which we organized the *Wisdom* symposium), and then as an outdoor May Day play three weeks later on May 5.

Our set designer preferred the May Day production, surrounded by its festive array of pageantry, games, and crafts. This place-and-scaffold performance enhanced the visual splendour of the play. Christ's gilded face and elegantly flowing robes were dazzling in the sunlight. Nevertheless, outdoors the play appealed to its viewers in a less subtle way. The expository opening dialogue—played indoors as a tender love scene between Wisdom and Anima—could not hold the outdoor audience, which responded more to the broad comic gestures in the interlude of sin. The play contains precise inversions of structure, costuming, and character as well as frequent verbal echoes, exemplified, for instance, by the word "game," a term which Anima uses to describe Wisdom's contemplative love for her (l. 40), and which is later echoed in the repeated "game" of lust (11. 603, 612). Such subtleties were lost in the open air. And without the banquet tables as props, references to "met and drynke" and exhortations to go to the "wyne" (see, for instance, ll. 813–27, 868) lost their immediate point, making it difficult to establish effective audience interaction.

In contrast, by setting the indoor performance as an abbot's banquet masque presented to King Edward IV on a visit to Bury St. Edmunds during Easter week of 1474, we established an occasion in which the audience became a part of the dramatic fiction. Using the description of Henry VI's earlier visit to Bury as a source, we began the event with a fealty ceremony for a costumed Edward IV and Queen Elizabeth in the Trinity Chapel. The "King" and "Queen" then led the audience in a procession to the banquet hall for the feast which preceded the play. Each succeeding decision neatly locked into this framework, confirming and re-confirming its plausibility. The aristocratic, masque-like quality of the play, its references to food and drink, the liturgical chants and processions, and the invocation of monastic ideals: these fitted well with the smallness of the playing space, the conviviality of feasters willing to be teased, and the fiction of placing an aristocratic audience in an abbot's Great Hall.

In the absence of historical performance records, we used the text itself as our primary production guide, confirming its suggestions about time, place, and audience when possible by the pictorial evidence of art history and the few records of monastic entertainment which remain. Relying heavily on the morality convention of audience admonition, we first decided on the banquet setting. Like most moralities, *Wisdom* points an accusing finger at its audience, implicating viewers in the actions of the dramatized sinners. Thus, the well-dressed feaster in the audience becomes an easy object of prey for characters tempted to covet riches and fine goods—a dramatic ploy consistent with the convention of inducing guilt in viewers as a key to repentance (while also, of course, entertaining them with the activities they are to be accused of enjoying).

Similarly, the three masque dances which occur in the center of *Wisdom* serve as emblems of sin. Each dance requires six dancers, liveried as followers of the renamed central characters: Mind/Maintenance, Understanding/Perjury, and Will/Lechery. These dances, which provide the play's only representation of the seven deadly sins, constitute a demonic anti-masque in the midst of the drama. As we conceptualized the dances, they began in a stately manner (as two rondes and one bransles) and then increasingly degenerated into the unlicensed disorder characteristic of the world under Lucifer's control.

Wisdom embodies the sense of dramatic stasis and the fixed, self-defining poses characteristic of choreographed allegory—of the masque or, before it, the disguising. The play begins with a long expository dialogue between Wisdom and Anima, followed by a liturgical procession of Anima's five virgin "wits," expository speeches of Anima's three faculties or "Mights," and a chanted recessional. But *Wisdom* also operates on a principle of dramatic opposition. Lucifer's world of sin opposes and inverts Christ's state of grace in a way that polarizes piety and sin. Structurally, the play sets liturgical processions in opposition to masque dances. The result is a courtly play which ironically attacks the value of courtly entertainment and redefines courtly pageantry in liturgical terms. The basic contrast is between divine unity and earthly fragmentation. The plainsong in the play symbolizes the wholeness and harmony of God's kingdom. In contrast, three-part music (the "tenowr," "mene," and "trebull" which the Mights sing as one of their first acts of sin, see 11. 617–20) and masque dancing signify the breaking of the universal wholeness of God. We accounted for the liturgical qualities and their masque-like counterparts by calling the play a "morality/masque" and by emphasizing the stately processional rhythm in the state of grace and the rhythm of the demonic anti-masque in the interlude of sin.

Though it served us well, the term "masque" is anachronistic in this context. The fifteenth-century term would have been "disguising," and that term is used twice in *Wisdom*, where it indicates costume as disguise. In his symposium paper (not in this volume), David Parry argued that characters ought to be masked throughout *Wisdom*. However, the play clearly calls for masks to be worn only by the dancers, and we used them only to mask characters in the interlude of sin, where each mask implied a moral judgment of the masked character. The term "dysgysynge" itself contains these moral overtones, for in addition to its sense of "disguise," it also means new-fangled clothing. Both senses occur in the play where the term designates, first, Anima's black mantle as a "disguise" of the soul's purity (l. 140) and, second, the dandy's "array"[2] with which Lucifer seduces the Mights.

After thus defining the genre of the play, we tackled the more problematic issues of time and place. Of these decisions, choosing a season of the year was the easiest. Like most moralities, *Wisdom* dramatizes the doctrine of penance, particularly appropriate for the Lenten season. More specifically, the text directs that one of the four chants be sung "wyth drawte notys as yt ys songyn in the passyon wyke" (stage direction after l. 996). This chant, "Velud mare contricio," is taken from the service for Maundy Thursday. Since this timing fits well with the penitential scheme (and, by the accident of Easter occurring late in April in 1984, with our production plans), we elected the Easter season.

This season accorded well with our desire to stake out a position on a more controversial issue—the possibility that *Wisdom* might have been performed in the Abbey of Bury St. Edmunds. In our symposium, Gail McMurray Gibson argued convincingly for Bury as a possible locus of the play (see p. 57). But, as Alexandra Johnston pointed out, identifying the manuscripts with the Abbey and assuming the play to have been performed there are different matters (see p. 96).

The main textual evidence for a monastic performance is the contemplative theme and the characterization of the Mights as cloistered monks. The play is framed by references to the contemplative tradition. Wisdom begins by quoting Heinrich Suso's *Orologium Sapien-*

tiae, a fourteenth-century treatise on wisdom translated into English in the fifteenth century. In his dialogue with Anima, Wisdom further draws on contemplative literature by summarizing the lower stages of contemplation as outlined by Walter Hilton in *The Scale of Perfection*, also a popular contemplative manual. Thus, Christ as Wisdom answers Anima's urgent questions about her own nature and her relationship to wisdom by invoking contemplative models.

It is true that Wisdom alludes only to Hilton's lower stages of contemplation in a dialogue that primarily reflects the sensuous love language of the Song of Songs. Considered alone, this scene would not have influenced us to stage the play in the Abbey of Bury St. Edmunds. But it is tied in with Lucifer's later addressing the Mights as "idle" cloistered contemplatives: "fonnyde fathers, founders of foly" (l. 393). This is one of the most controversial sections of the play, for in this scene alone, the Mights seem to be cast as monks, who are being urged by the play to resist Lucifer's temptations and, thus, to renew their commitment to a cloistered life. Throughout this scene, Lucifer's temptations all have to do with entering the world. First, in answer to Mind's affirmation of the contemplative life ("Contemplatyff lyff ys sett befor," l. 417), he holds up the model of the Vita Mixta (or mixed life), which he says "Gode here began" (l. 428). In the same vein, Lucifer urges the Mights to "Be in the world, vse thyngys nesesse" (l. 442); he encourages Understanding to leave "all syngler deuocyons" (l. 452) in order to take delight in the world. Will is urged to "lewe his nyse chastyte and take a wyff" (l. 476). In this scene the monastic associations are clear; arguments to the contrary—for instance, that "fathers" could designate secular magnates as well as clerics,[3] or that Will lives a celi-

WISDOM

bate life because he is a student[4]–might individually be persuasive, but they lose their strength in the context of the whole scene, which echoes the same theme time after time: Lucifer is tempting a set of cloistered contemplatives to enter the world.

Acting on this evidence, which fits well with the liturgical character of the opening and closing scenes and may help to explain why masque dances are used in the play only as emblems of sinfulness, we elected the monastic setting for the play. However, we rejected the possibility of a closed monastic performance. The text implies a mixed audience. When tempting Mind, Lucifer singles out an audience member whom he identifies as a man "that lywyt worldly,/Hathe wyffe, chylderne, and serwantys besy" (ll. 405–06). As our Lucifer played the part, he then suggests illicit, adulterous obligations: "And other chargys that I not specyfye" (l. 407). To make this moment of comedy work well, the audience must contain non-religious members in circumstances which also make sense of Lucifer's attack on the cloistered life, as, for example, an audience of aristocratic guests in an Abbot's Great Hall.

Where does all this leave us with regard to staging? So far, our evidence has justified a banquet morality/masque which might be set in a monastery though almost certainly not played only before monks. The kinds of aristocratic entertainment with which *Wisdom* belongs would in those circumstances be found, if in a monastery at all, only in the Abbot's Palace–provided perhaps for visiting dignitaries. But who and when? These questions led us to focus more closely on the iconography of costuming. Fortunately, the play contains detailed costume descriptions for each character. These directions consistently establish the metaphor of feudal livery as a sign of allegiance: the Mights are "crested in Anima's sute" (direction after l. 324); each of the dancing companies is "dysgysde in the sute" of its patron (direction after l. 692). Costuming directions also emphasize the royalty of Wisdom and Anima:

> Fyrst enteryde WYSDOME in a ryche purpull clothe of golde wyth a mantyll of the same ermynnyde wythin, hawynge abowt hys neke a ryall hood furred wyth ermyn, wpon hys hede a cheweler wyth browys, a berde of golde of sypres curlyed, a ryche imperyall crown þerwpon sett wyth precyus stonys and perlys, in hys leyfte honde a balle of golde wyth a cros þerwppon and in hys ryght honde a regall schepter. (Opening stage direction)

To be sure, portraying Christ as Emperor is a conventional theological emblem.[5] And the sovereignty of God is a theme in other morality plays, as for instance in *The Castle of Perseverance*. But in that play, as in *Mundus et Infans*, royal clothing has vulgar connotations, indicating vanity not divinity, and feudal livery serves only as a metaphor for sin.[6] In contrast, in *Wisdom* royal robes signify divinity, and feudal livery provides the metaphor for loyalty to good and bad masters.

Here the play makes visually clear the underlying assumption of our production: the iconography of power and authority points simultaneously in two directions, inward to spiritual truth and outward to the many points of intersection which existed between political and theological discourse. The King is robed in garments which recall those of God the sovereign ruler, and Christ is clothed in a way that inevitably calls to mind the English king. The fabrics of Christ's costume were, in fact, restricted by custom and law to the English royal family. In the 1480s, sumptuary laws specifically limited both ermine and royal purple cloth of gold to members of the King's immediate family, his wife, children, and siblings. These laws codified clothing restrictions maintained throughout the century.

The point may best be illustrated by two portraits of royalty (see plates 1 and 2). The first portrait depicts Christ as "Eternal Wisdom" and is taken from a fifteenth century manuscript of the German works of Heinrich Suso, whose *Orologium Sapientiae* served as a source for *Wisdom*. Here Christ is clothed almost precisely as in the play. In plate 2, Edward IV sits enthroned and surrounded by those paying homage to him in a pose reminiscent of that of Christ in the Suso woodcut. He, too, wears an ermine-lined purple cloth of gold mantle, a royal hood, a rich imperial crown. He, too, holds the "balle" in his left hand and the sceptre in his right.[7]

Similarly, Anima's costume has regal connotations which have been ignored in the critical literature. In the play, she is identified as Wisdom's spouse, an identification affirmed by her clothing at the beginning of the play:

> Here entrethe ANIMA as a mayde, in a wyght clothe of golde gysely purfyled wyth menyver, a mantyll of blake þerwppeon, a cheueler lyke to WYSDOM, wyth a ryche chappelet lasyde behynde hangynge down wyth to knottys of golde and syde tasselys, knelynge down to WYSDOM. (stage direction after l. 16)

Except for the slightly puzzling long tassels and gold

WISDOM

"knottys," this costume iconographically signifies the purity of the soul under the cover of a mantle of sin. The costume also indicates Anima's royal status. Though in chaste white rather than royal purple, Anima is essentially garbed in the livery of Christ: fur-lined cloth of gold robe and gilded wig "lyke to Wysdom"; her chappelet becomes a crown at the end of the play. Moreover, there is a fascinating parallel between Anima's costume and the clothes traditionally worn by the English royal consort on the eve of her coronation. According to the "Little Device for the Coronation of Henry VII," a document which pre-dates Henry's reign, the Queen takes a penitential ride on the eve of her coronation. For that ride, she is to be:

> arayed in a kirtel of white damaske cloth of gold furred with myniuer pur ... a Mantell ... with a greit lase and ii botons and taxselles of white silke and gold.

For iconographic purposes which are specifically designated in the play, Anima wears a black rather than a white mantle. Otherwise, her attire is precisely that of the Queen in a pre-coronation ritual of penance. Both wear white cloth of gold robes furred with miniver. Anima wears a "chappelet"; the Queen, a circle of gold around her head. Even Anima's two buttons of gold and long tassels find a referent in the Queen's "ii botons and taxselles of white silke and gold." In short, Anima's costume as a penitent soul suggests royal marriage as well as her role as the spouse of Wisdom; and to make this point clear we doubled the costumes of Anima and Edward IV's Queen for our production.

In order to emphasize Lucifer's nature as a kind of anti-Wisdom, we clothed him in black satin robes, with large dangling bat-like claws, rather than in the more usual bestial costume. These black robes were

WISDOM

foreshadowed by Anima's black mantle in the opening scene and then echoed again in the foul costume in which she appears after the interlude of sin. The Mights, too, dress in Lucifer's livery in the interlude of sin. But their clothes reflect the initial attractiveness of sin, in contrast to Anima's costume which reflects the actual ugliness of the sinful state. In order to seduce the Mights without scaring them, Lucifer changes into—or rather takes off his devil's "array" to reveal beneath—a gallant's disguise. When they move from grace to sinfulness, the Mights, too, change their long robes (their "syde array") for a similar dandy's "dysgysynge." Again, the play's clothing metaphor—the change from long to short robes—has topical implications, linking the court and the church in mutually conservative efforts in a way that worked well with our central hypothesis. From the mid-fourteenth century on, long robes were increasingly associated with two groups of people: clerics and the king's associates. In an attempt to prevent the change in style from long to short clothes, fifteenth-century sumptuary laws forbade (apparently with little effect) the wearing of short garments, which were considered indecent. One such set of laws was passed in 1463, approximately the time when *Wisdom* may have been composed.

 The opposition between Wisdom and Lucifer seen in dramatic structure and costuming dominates this play, even in the staging. The interlude of sin is set in the banquet hall, with the tables as props for the actors, who interact regularly with the audience. In contrast, Wisdom's state of grace is set in infinite space and eternal time. Only when he descends from the throne to deliver his homily on the nine points of wisdom does Wisdom acknowledge the assembled crowd.

Otherwise, the drama divides between the human world of Lucifer and the infinite kingdom of God.

Our conception of the play, however, collapsed the distinction between "universal" allegory and topical satire. Though set in infinite time, Wisdom's kingdom reflects the conservative orthodoxy of the fifteenth century and, in this sense, has social and political overtones of its own. There are many ways to depict a timeless kingdom of God. Choosing images that mirror one's earthly ideals identifies social and political as well as theological aspirations. For instance, modern fundamentalist assumptions that heaven's streets are filled with gold and that all the angels live in gilded age mansions reflect the aspirations of early twentieth-century Christians. In much the same way, the depiction of Wisdom's kingdom as a place where the redeemed wear old-fashioned long robes, sing only plainsong chants, and prefer liturgical processions to masque dances makes a statement about the conservative nature of both theological and social ideals in the fifteenth century. The nostalgic backward-looking quality of a play like *Wisdom* serves a dual purpose: both to reinforce orthodox Christianity in a period of conservative reform and to insinuate through costuming, language, and structure the alliance between Christian orthodoxy and monarchical authority.

Such a dual perspective involves, of course, a level of sublimation in a play like *Wisdom*. The English king is nowhere named in the play, but the play's ideals of kingship and conservative aristocratic style imply the need for absolute obedience to the king, whether divine or secular. And, as a matter of fact, in a period in which royal favor often helped to counteract the influence of powerful local landlords, such an idealization may have served practical purposes as well.

In his relationship with the town of Bury, the Abbot of Bury St. Edmunds was much like any other powerful landlord attempting to hold onto his sphere of influence against persistent local challenges. In their recurrent battles to retain control over the town of Bury and to maintain jurisdictional independence from visitations by the Bishop of Norwich, Edmundsbury abbots did court English kings. Henry VI had a special relationship to the Abbey, spending the Christmas and Easter seasons of 1433–34 in the residences of the prior and the abbot. Abbot William Curteys rebuilt the abbot's palace for this extensive visit, descriptions of which served as a model for much of our ceremony.[8] Later, Henry held two parliaments in Bury during the 1440s. As Gail Gibson has pointed out, Edward IV initially had no such relationship with the abbey, but in an effort to avoid disfavor incurred by the Lancastrian alliance, the abbey courted Edward's favor. Edward projected a visit in 1474, which he apparently did not make, though he did visit East Anglia in that year. In such circumstances, a powerful cleric like the Abbot of Bury St. Edmunds would have assumed a burden of entertainment similar to that provided by other aristocratic hosts. Under these circumstances, a play like *Wisdom* might well have been—as Gibson conjectured—the abbot's gift to the king.

This, at least, was the hypothesis which served as the basis for our major staging decisions. The only problem with this assumption is that there is not much support in the few extant monastic records for the performance of plays like *Wisdom* in an abbey like that at Bury. As cited by Alexandra Johnston, the scant references to payments for plays at Bury all come from the early sixteenth century and, in every instance, record payments for players coming into the abbey to perform. (See p. 97).

What does this kind of evidence do to our major thesis? It can mean, as Johnston suggested, that *Wisdom* might have been written by a monk of Bury not for the abbey but for a local landlord. Or it could mean, as Donald Baker argued, that *Wisdom* might well have been a traveling play; though the formidable array of dancers—twelve at least—and the odd fact that Wisdom and Lucifer cannot easily be doubled probably indicate that this play was not in the regular repertoire of a small professional troupe. But there is another possibility—one suggested in passing by Johnston: that *Wisdom* was performed at the abbey but by players from one of the local great houses.

Such a hypothesis makes sense, especially when one looks again at those detailed costuming directions. *Wisdom* is elegantly costumed. It requires skilled musicians and its dancers must be able to perform masque dances. But there are no staging devices. The play is without the kinds of machinery that frequently accompanied the later masque: there are no worlds on wheels, no fiery heavens, no stage devices. This may be simply because of the nature of the play. But it is also true that costumes travel easily; stage machinery does not. A group of performers from a nearby estate could easily bring with them costumes for a play like *Wisdom*; they might have more trouble transporting large-scale stage machinery.

Putting all this evidence together, there is finally no way to resolve the question of monastic performance. But there are large areas of agreement: *Wisdom* is a banquet play; it is masque-like; and it was probably played before an aristocratic audience which included some religious. For the rest, perhaps finally we should admit that the issue is not as large as it seems. *Wisdom* does idealize the contemplative life. But in the fifteenth century that idealization need not have the monastery as its main focus. By this time lay spirituality had adopted many of the features of monastic piety. John Dahmus, writing of fifteenth-century Germany, defines the way in which conservative, essentially monastic ideals were being imposed upon laymen. When one remembers the flowering of lay contemplation in England during the fifteenth century and the extent to which manuals like the *Scale of Perfection* and *Orologium Sapientiae* were used by lay men and women, it is obvious that his remarks are also applicable to fifteenth-century England:

> ... the layman was being asked to deny his own world, ironically at the very time when the powerful force of humanism was questioning the traditional view of man and the cosmos. The layman was being refused first-class citizenship in the kingdom of heaven unless he became, in effect, a monk. A layman was an imperfect Christian because ... only religious men and women could live a perfect Christian life.[9]

This, I would suggest, is essentially what *Wisdom* demands: that laymen accept a concept of spirituality which is best suited to the cloisters. At the same time, the play does also insist that acts of charity are not incompatible with Christian perfection. Whether it was set in the abbot's Great Hall before the king or in the home of the Duke of Norfolk before visiting monks,[10] the play tells its viewers that the only real path to wisdom is that of personal renunciation of worldly pleasures and acquisitions. Against Lucifer's world of raucous cunning, the play holds up an ascetic ideal of obedience grounded in contemplative love. But this love is elegant and beautiful; the world of sin, for all its comic interplay, is finally vulgar.

As we conceptualized it, *Wisdom* clearly finds its place in the fifteenth-century conservative effort to forestall the modern world. That effort brought about alliances between ecclesiastical and secular interests. It was to dramatize this assumption that we elected to hold our feast inside the monastery of Bury St. Edmunds and to show the play as flattering the reigning—and perhaps visiting—monarch.

NOTES

1. For instance, Mark Eccles in his edition of the play says that "*Wisdom* is too intent on teaching moral virtue to have much concern with dramatic virtues." See *The Macro Plays*, EETS, o.s., no. 262 (London: Oxford University Press, 1969), p. xxxvi. In his review of the 1981 Winchester Cathedral production of *Wisdom*, Peter Happé similarly calls *Wisdom* a "strangely limited" drama which fails "to integrate the ideas about law and politics which are present in the text" (*RORD*, 24, 1981, 197). All quotations from *Wisdom* in the present article are taken from the Eccles edition.

2. The terms "dysgysynge" and "aray" are opposites in the play, as suggested by Wisdom in his explication of Anima's costume ("Yowr dysgysynge and yowr aray," 1. 150). Used in this context, "aray" indicates the natural condition or designates costume which identifies the fealty allegiance of a character. For a discussion of such language as used in *The Castle of Perseverance*, see

WISDOM

Milla Riggio, "The Allegory of Feudal Acquisition in *The Castle of Perseverance*," in Morton Bloomfield, ed., *Allegory, Myth and Symbol*, Harvard English Studies, 9 (1981), p. 193.

3. Johnston, "*Wisdom* and the Records," p.95. See also J. J. Molloy, *A Theological Interpretation of the Moral Play Wisdom, Who Is Christ* (Washington, D. C. 1952), p. 77.
4. Baker, p. 80.
5. See Bevington, p. 22.
6. See Riggio, pp. 194-198.
7. Plate 1 is taken from Codex Guelf. 78.5 fol. 97r°, Wolfenbüttel. Photograph supplied by Gerhard Strasser, reproduced by permission of the Anton Herzog Library. Plate 2 shows William, Lord Herbert, and Anne, his wife, kneeling before Edward IV. From the *Troy Book* by John Lydgate, British Museum Royal MS 18 D II, fol. 6.
8. See William Dugdale, *Monasticon Anglicanum* (London: James Bohn, 1846), III, 113. Dugdale reports that during Henry VI's 1433-34 visit to the Abbey of Bury St. Edmunds "an altercation once more arose between the bishop of Norwich and the abbat, respecting jurisdiction." This altercation was, perhaps predictably, settled in favor of the abbot (p. 115).
9. John Dahmus, "Preaching to the Laity in Fifteenth-Century Germany: Johannes Nider's 'Harps,'" *Journal of Ecclesiastical History*, 34 (1983), 62-63.
10. Johnston suggests the Howards, Dukes of Norfolk, or John de la Pole, second Duke of Suffolk, as possible secular patrons of *Wisdom*, see p.100-01.

"Blake and wyght, fowll and fayer": Stage Picture in *Wisdom*

DAVID M. BEVINGTON

Walter Hilton's *Scale of Perfection*, written in English in Nottinghamshire before 1396, is a major source for the play of *Wisdom Who Is Christ* and in particular for lines 103–70 that form the opening dialogue between Wisdom or Christ as King and Anima, the soul of man. Hilton's text describes the relation between these two figures in terms that bear important implications for a theater of visualized moral abstraction. What do the qualities of soul look like in the theater? How is the soul to be rendered in contrastive theatrical modes as it resembles both God and the devil? Hilton offers a visual vocabulary that repeatedly stresses the dual concept of *image* and *likeness*. Every soul "is the ymage of God," says Hilton, quoting 1 Corinthians 11:7. The soul is "made to the ymage and to the lyknes of hym," "wonderly fayre." Conversely, however, through man's fall in Adam, the "lyknes" of man has been "dysfygured." As a result, the "soule of a chylde that is borne and is uncrystenyd by cause of orygynal synne" is "nought but an ymage of the fende & a bronde of helle." This defacement can be remedied alone through Christ's sacrifice and through the individual's baptism, whereby the soul is "reformed & restored to the fyrst lyknes"; but man's sensual nature is quick to undo this good. Sensuality, defined by Hilton as "flesshly felynge by the fyve outwarde wyttes," that is, the part of the soul concerned with the physical senses, can readily become the means through which the soul loses and inverts its likeness to God. When man's sensual nature "is unskylfully and unordynatly ruled," it "is made the ymage of synne." Reason accordingly has two parts: the "over partye" or higher part which is "propyrly the ymage of god" and the "neyther" or lower part through which the soul understands the use of earthly things. "Fayr is mannes soule & fowle is a mannes soule," Hilton summarizes, "foule without as it were a beest / fayre within lyke to an angel."[1]

This oxymoronic language of contrastive likeness is insistently placed before us in the text of *Wisdom*. Anima introduces herself as "I that represent here þe sowll of man," and wants to know from Wisdom what constitutes the soul. Wisdom answers: "Yt ys þe ymage of Gode þat all began; / And not only ymage, but hys lyknes 3e are" (ll. 101–4). This image took upon it "þe fylthe of synne orygynall" at Adam's fall (ll. 109–11), and every soul since is transformed in likeness. "For 3e be dysvyguryde be hys synne," Wisdom explains to Anima (1. 117). The soul can be reformed "to hys fyrste lyght" only through Christ's sacrifice and the seven sacraments, first through baptism that does "wasche away" and "clensythe" original sin. This sacrament

> reformyt þe sowll in feythe verray
> To þe gloryus lyknes of Gode eternall
> And makyt yt as fayer and as celestyall
> As yt neuer dyffowlyde had be. (127–30)

Sensuality, defined as in Hilton as fleshly perception ("felynge") attended on by the five wits or senses, "Ys made þe ymage of synne then of hys foly," and, though Reason is defined contrastingly as "þe ymage of Gode propyrly," the "neyther" part of Reason must learn to agree with bodily appetite (ll. 140–48). These "tweyn," Reason and Sensuality, do thereby signify

> Yowr dysgysynge and yowr aray,
> Blake and wyght, fowll and fayer vereyly. (150–1)

Every soul is black "by sterynge of synne þat cummyth all-day," and is also white "by knowenge of reson veray" (ll. 153, 155).

> Thus a sowle ys bothe fowlle and fayer:
> Fowll as a best be felynge of synne,
> Fayer as a angell, of hewyn þe ayer. (ll. 157–59)

The fifteenth-century morality play, I intend to argue here, derives its theatrical form from the visualizing of metaphor, from the concretizing of homiletic and scriptural proposition. Of course the morality play had the considerable advantage in this matter of finding metaphors already fully expanded in narrative form in poems like *Le Chasteau d'Amour*, in the visual arts, and in tracts like the *Scale of Perfection*, but the structural importance of metaphor as the very basis of dramatic form nonetheless should not be minimized in our attempt to understand how the morality genre came into being on the medieval stage. *Mankind* (ca. 1465–70) takes its form from the military metaphor embedded in Job 7:1: "Þer is euer a batell betwyx the soull and the body: *Vita hominis est milicia super terram*" (ll. 227–28). *The Castle of Perseverance* (ca. 1400–25) visualizes a similar metaphor, with obvious indebtedness to the *Psychomachia* of Prudentius and to the *Chasteau d'Amour*, of a besieged castle; it also makes important use of the metaphoric verse from Psalms 84:11 (85:10 in the English King James version), "*Misericordia et Veritas obviaverunt sibi; Justitia et Pax osculatae sunt*, Mercy and Truth have met together; Righteousness and Peace have kissed each other." The proposition that human life is a journey or pilgrimage is evident in early morality plays such as *Everyman* (ca. 1495) in which the protagonist's friends fall away from him as he approaches death. The summoning of Death is a metaphor visualized in this play and in *The Castle of Perseverance*. I suggest that the informing metaphor to be visualized in *Wisdom* is one of image or likeness that alters radically between white and black or fair and foul. The opening passage of the play spells out in homiletic terms what will be enacted and visualized. The emphasis on "dysgysynge" (i.e., symbolic costuming), disfiguring, defiling, cleansing, reforming, and the like helps explain a number of staging devices: the attentiveness to contrastive costuming, the omnipresence of costuming alterations, the use of symmetry in the arrangement of characters and stage picture, the contrastive grouping of large numbers of extras, and the lack of a central psychomachia figure other than the ambiguous and passive Anima.

WISDOM

The great exception in this play to the otherwise universal motif of contrastive costuming is Wisdom himself or Christ as king. Wisdom's entrance marks the start of the play with a royal appearance like that of the royal entry in a tournament or civic pageant. Wisdom appears

> in a ryche purpull clothe of golde wyth a mantyll of the same ermynnyde wythin, hawynge abowt hys neke a ryall hood furred wyth ermyn, wpon hys hede a cheweler wyth browys, a berde of golde of sypres curlyed, a ryche imperyall crown Þerwpon sett wyth precyus stonys and perlys, in hys leyfte honde a balle of golde wyth a cros Þerwppon and in hys ryght honde a regall schepter.

This figure resembles both Christ enthroned in the van Eyck Ghent Altarpiece and fifteenth-century English kings as they are iconographically represented in contemporary illustrations (see plates 2–4, 7). We see an image of Christ as wise and triumphant ruling monarch, an image that persists into the late Middle Ages and Early Renaissance (as the van Eyck altarpiece attests) despite the increasing emphasis in Gothic art on the Man of Sorrows. Wisdom's very name bespeaks his royalty: it is, he says, a "nayme imperyall," one that entitles him to be "clepyde of hem Þat in erthe be / Euerlastynge Wysdom" (ll. 3–4). His name thus stresses the immeasurable gap between his high majesty, enthroned in heaven, and those who dwell below on earth. His name is "to my nobley egalle," equal to my nobleness. Although the name pertains to the second person of the Trinity, it envisages him as ruler, serene and mighty, receiving tribute and sitting in judgment. This emphasis is derived from the treatise on which these particular lines is based, the *Orologium Sapientiae*.[2]

Staging choices reinforce the verbal emphasis on Christ's majestic status that sets him apart from his lowly subjects. His costume is dominantly purple cloth of gold trimmed with white, in visible distinction to the black and white contrast of all creatures here below. Ermine, equated with royalty, trims his mantle and his "ryall hood." Wig, artificial eyebrows, and curled cloth-of-gold beard lend to the head a masklike impassive timeless quality associated, as in the van Eyck painting, with the Romanesque style. The crown is richly decorated with gems, as in the van Eyck painting, and the insignia of office are in Christ's hands. Although the stage directions do not so specify, a throne would seem to be required.

Christ's figurative and literal centrality in the opening scene suggests the iconography of Last Judgment art and drama, where Christ appears majestically in his second coming to judge mankind. Horizontal symmetry and vertical hierarchy are prominently developed, as in Judgment art, to distinguish left from right and ascent from descent. Christ bears in his left hand the cross or token of his passion and in his right hand the regal scepter. Throughout the play we are provided with symmetrically balanced tableaus, as when the restored Anima enters "wyth þe Fyve Wyttys goynge before, Mynde on þe on syde and Wndyrstongynge on þe other syde and Wyll folowyng, all in here fyrst clothynge, her chapplettys and crestys, and all hauyng on crownys" (l. 1064). Symmetry is, like costume change, a visual key to the dialectic of good and evil with which the play is concerned.

At the same time, Wisdom shares the physical center of the play with a very different figure, that of Anima. I have elsewhere discussed how Anima is the focus of a casting scheme that enables a group of

WISDOM

actors to double parts between good and evil and thereby project an image of man's dual nature that is alternately serious and comic.[3] My interest here is a complementary one, not in casting but in visualization of metaphor through costume, properties, gestures, stage movement, grouping, and the like. In these terms, Anima is no less the central figure than is Wisdom or Christ. That is to say, all the visual oppositions of the play, as in the spectacles of the three mights and their followers, are physically expressive of Anima's dual nature. *The Castle of Perseverance* is also symmetrical, but it is controlled by metaphors of conflict rather than of visible contrast between black and white, foul and fair, outer and inner. As a result, Anima's long silences and the emptiness of her characterization noted by critics become less of a problem in visual terms, for she is often expressively the center of the scene even when she has no speaking part.

The pairing with Wisdom at the visual center of the play and of the acting arena is instructive, for Anima is, we are repeatedly told, made in God's "ymage" or "lyknes." Yet in what sense is this true? Christ is robed in purple cloth of gold, every inch a king; Anima is the spouse of Christ, appropriately wigged as a queen, and yet she is also a "mayde" dressed visibly in black and white. She is costumed in "wyght clothe of golde gysely purfyled wyth menyver," that is, white cloth of gold handsomely bordered with white fur signifying her majesty, and yet she also wears "a mantyll of blake þerwppeon." Her wig or "cheueler" is "lyke to Wysdom, wyth a ryche chappelet [headdress] lasyde behynde hangynge down with to knottys of golde and syde [long] tasselys" (following l. 16). But the striking feature of her garb is the contrast between inner purity and outward contamination.[4] She kneels to Wis-

WISDOM

dom, properly stressing in visual terms her lowliness as compared to his might. The dialogue, moreover, repeatedly stresses the incomparable nature of his Godhead: "Wysdom," he says, "ys better þan all worldly precyosnes, / And all þat may dysyryde be / Ys not in comparyschon to my lyknes" (ll. 33–35). Anima truly speaks of him as "Godhede incomprehensyble" (l. 94). The sense in which the soul is a likeness or image of God, then, is visibly qualified. No one on earth can even know God's likeness, much less embody it, but humans may, "By knowynge of yowrsylff...haue felynge / Wat Gode ys in yowr sowle sensyble" (ll. 95–96). The soul can never aspire to what is regal or imperial in God's majesty, that is, to what is manifested as purple, but the soul's whiteness within is godly. White symbolizes the purity through which mankind takes joy in God; it is by "clene" souls only that God loves to be "halsyde and kyssyde of mankynde" (ll. 44–45). His love "dyschargethe and puryfyethe clene" the burden of sin in those who seek him, redeeming "pure" those who are troubled by the "fylthe and ordure" of worldly "lustys and lykyngys" (ll. 51–55). The contrast of whiteness and filth is established early in this play, in costuming and in dialogue, as the polar antithesis around which the play is structured.

Once the antithesis has been established in the costuming of the central figure, Anima, the play proceeds through abstraction to objectify and illustrate in the theater the proposition of man's dual being. Such a scheme calls for elaborate symmetries, and is assisted in this play by a sizeable cast of nonspeaking extras. Five virgins attend on Anima, representing her five "Wyttys" or senses. Mind, Understanding, and Will are each attended by six retainers who appear one after the other to illustrate the worldly corruption of the soul's three attributes. Probably seven (the manuscript reads six) small boys run out from under the horrible mantle of the soul "in þe lyknes of dewyllys" representing the seven Deadly Sins (following l. 912) and are eventually exorcised by contrition. In her restored condition, the Soul is attended on by the five wits in procession. As before, I am interested here not in the significant potential of doubling of at least some of these nonspeaking extras and hence the way in which doubling patterns lend themselves to symmetrical contrast between good and evil, but rather in the symbolic meaning of the oppositions. In all these groups of extras we find visual oxymoron, inherent contradiction, expressed through contrastive costuming that pits one group against another. Such oxymoron is necessary because the groups of extras objectivize the contradictory and amphibian nature of the play's central psychomachia figure.

The five virgins attending on Anima first enter "in white kertyllys and mantelys, wyth cheuelers and chappelyttys, and synge 'Nigra sum sed formosa, filia Jerusalem, sicut tabernacula cedar et sicut pelles Salamonis'" (l. 164).[5] Their singing from the Song of Songs (1.4) introduces their relation to Anima in terms of the opposition between outer and inner, dark and fair; as she interprets the verse, the daughters of Jerusalem do not find fault with her "For þis dyrke schadow I bere of humanyte, / That as þe tabernacull of cedar wythowt yt ys blake / Ande wythine as þe skyn of Salamone full of bewty" (ll. 165–68). In the words of the Song of Songs, again, Anima asks that she not be looked down on "Quod fusca sum," because I am dark, having been discolored or scorched by the sun. If the five wits or senses keep the Soul "clene" and never "deface" it, "Godys ymage neuer xall ryve," be riven, and the "clene sowll" will remain in "Godys restynge place" (ll. 174–76).

The five wits are thus introduced in terms of the opposition between outer and inner; it is by the "fyve wyttys bodyly" that Anima drifts into temptation, ignoring the counsel of "my inwarde wyttys, thow ben gostly" (ll. 1074–76). The "prudent vyrgins" attending on Anima do not, however, share her disguise. They are essentially liveried in her white and gold; the stage direction at line 164 makes no mention of black.[6] The playwright makes no attempt to signal their dual nature through a costume change that would sign their fall from grace, as he does with the three Mights. Instead, the five wits disappear from the stage entirely during the lively scenes of temptation. Iconographically, they are perhaps associated with the wise virgins of the *Sponsus* play (twelfth century), a subject with explicitly eschatalogical overtones. Like the wise virgins of that play, these five virgins dressed predominantly in white are identified with Anima's purity; they appear with her only during her initial stage of innocence and then during her recovery to contrition at the play's very end. They commence their long and significant absence by exiting in procession at line 324, singing "Tota pulcra es" from the Song of Songs, "You are beautiful, my dearest, beautiful without a flaw" (4.7), a text sung as an antiphon for the procession on Trinity Sunday in the Sarum Missal.[7] The five wits are thus linked to liturgical procession, to liturgical song, to the iconography of the wise virgins in the *Sponsus*, to the imagery of Christ as a bride or "worthy spowse" (l. 69), to order and ceremony, to beauty, love, and purity. Their exit in liturgical procession at line 324 signals the end of

WISDOM

purity and the commencement of foul defacement.

The presentational signals in the mummings of the retainers of Mind, Understanding, and Will conversely emphasize disguise, disfigurement, and caricature. "Here entur six dysgysyde in þe sute of Mynde," reads the stage direction at line 692, and the third such stage direction also makes a point of disguising: "Here entreth six women in sut, thre dysgysyde as galontys and thre as matrones" following line 752. The opulent convention of the courtly mumming lends itself to such a vocabulary of pretense, for the mumming was known as a "disguising." Mumming also gives depth of meaning to the masks that are so prominently in use. The six jurors of Understanding are "vyseryde dyuersly" following line 724, while the retainers of Will appear "wyth wondyrfull vysurs congruent" or corresponding to their conditions following line 752. Masks or visors are thus the suitable facial covering for a "disguising" while they are also suggestive of false show. The visors of Understanding suggest the double faces of perjured jurors;[8] Understanding in fact introduces them as "Jorowrs in on hoode" that "beer to facys" (l. 718). The musical signals are similarly appropriate both to a courtly mumming and to a display of sinful excess: Mynde's "mynstrallys" or musicians are trumpeters, Understanding is heralded by a bagpipe, and Will by a hornpipe. The appurtenances in each case are those of merriment, unseemly dance, and riotous excess. Will explains to his retinue, "Yowr mynstrell a hornepype mete /Þat fowll ys in hymselff but to þe erys swete" (ll. 757–58), appealing to the conventional association of horn with cuckoldry.

Costuming is that of the antimasque, in vivid colors symbolically appropriate to sin and contrastive to the simple white of the cleansed soul. Mind's retainers appear in red beards (compared by Molloy to the red beard of Judas in the cycle plays)[9] with lions rampant on their crests. Red may well be present in their livery as well, as the color of blood appropriate to wrath. Lions are familiar symbols of pride,[10] and livery is here associated with the contemporary abuse of maintenance or protection of one's followers from the law of the realm.[11] The color red thus suits a dramatic parody of the abuse of power. Understanding's jurors are in judicial gowns, hoods, and "hattys of meyntenance," again pointing to the abuse of livery for maintenance. Will's six retainers are disguised as gallants and women, in pairs, to stress the fleshly and sensual nature of their entertainment; the terms "galontys" and "matrones" suggest wanton extravagance in costuming.

All is symbolic in these successive appearances of bands of retainers, even the numbers: "Seven ys a numbyr of dyscorde and inperfyghtnes" (l. 697), Mynde explains, and is of course the number of the Deadly Sins. Six retainers plus the leader produce seven revelers in each mumming show. Considerable stress is also placed on the number three, as in Wyll's explanation of Mynde's entourage that "Thes meny thre synnys comprehende: Pryde, Invy, and Wrathe in hys hettys" (ll. 715–16). The importance of symbolic numerology is related to an emphasis in all these mummings on dance, for the retainers arrange themselves in patterned movement, and each mumming is spoken of as a dance pattern. "Now wyll I than begyn my traces" (or dance steps), Understanding insists (l. 717), and Wyll makes a similar transition: "Now Meyntnance and Perjury / Hathe schewyde þe trace [series of steps in dancing] of þer cumpeny, / Ye xall se a sprynge [lively dance] of Lechery, /Þat to me attende" (ll. 745–48). The show of the three groups of retainers is both a dance and a dumb show: "Now wyll we thre do make a dance," says Mynde, "Off thow þat longe to owr retenance, / Cummynge in by contenance" (ll. 685–87). "By contenance" means that the eighteen dancers convey meaning through "contenance" only, that is, through gesture and movement.

These groups of dancers, with their lively antics, vivid costumes, symbolic numbers, and the like, offer visual contrast to the virgins of Anima whom they have replaced on stage during the middle portion of this morality play, the portion devoted to comic depravity and fall from grace. Antic dance replaces liturgical procession. Trumpets, bagpipes, and hornpipes replace the chanting of "Nigra sum sed formosa" and "Tota pulcra es" from the Song of Songs. Hats of maintenance replace chaplets of purity. The sluttish women who dance with their gallants in the retinue of Will are much like the foolish virgins of the *Sponsus*, in contrast to the five wise virgins who process with Anima. Following the courtly form of the antimasque, mumming and revelry replace religious devotion. Variety, color, and noise replace sobriety and decorum. The contrasts are perhaps all the more evident because they are conveyed presentationally, that is, entirely without speaking parts for the extras. *Wisdom* is unusual in the extent to which it relies on the visual and musical juxtaposition of groups of extras.

The seven small boys who run out from under the horrible mantle of the Soul and return again, later to be exorcised by Wisdom, are part of this same visual juxtaposition of groups of nonspeaking extras. The numbers are again symbolically suggestive, the costumes appropriate to antimasque. Small boys are chosen perhaps as a matter of staging convenience, for all must fit under Anima's mantle. Their foray into the acting arena and possibly into the audience is like that in the Anglo-Norman *Jeu d'Adam* where devils frequently sally forth among the spectators. They are no doubt theatrically entertaining, and yet their association with disfigurement is more stark than that of the three bands of retainers. They do not dance to pleasing music and do not play the role of human masquers at a court entertainment; they are "in þe lyknes of dewyllys" and prompt Wisdom to chide the Soul for having "made the a bronde of hell / Whom I made þe ymage of lyght" (ll. 917–18). The image of God is "defowlyde" (l. 927), requiring the strong "medsyne" (l. 970) of contrition to render "clene" (l. 954) again that which is foul. This retinue, in other words, is suited to the phase of the morality in which sin is recognized for the ugly thing it is rather than for the fair exterior it has usurped through masking—both figurative and literal masking. With the exorcising of the demons comes a voiding of "þe deullys blake" and of "Dedly synne" (ll. 979–80). Their expulsion signals the return of Anima to a responsiveness to grace.

In the presentational effects I have analyzed so far, costume change has played no part. The groups of extras achieve their symbolic statements through juxtaposition of dissimilar effects. Hence the dramatic form is one of alternation. Among the speaking characters, on the other hand, with the essential exception of Wisdom, who remains unaltered, change is manifested through substitution of costume. The visual metaphor is one of spiritual journey. Since costume announces who a character is, spiritually and morally, alternation in spiritual or moral status demands visual expression through new garments.

Such a language of moral meaning can be abused through evil intent, of course. Lucifer represents this perversion of moral language through a change of costuming that does not accompany moral change. He first appears, as the stage direction specifies, "in a dewyllys aray wythowt and wythin as a prowde galonte" (l. 325). The duality of inner and outer is obviously related to the motif of fair and foul, white and black as it appears elsewhere in the play. Yet the seeming resemblance is deceptive, for Lucifer is not, like Anima, fair within and foul without to signify the soul's potential cleanness and the flesh's corrupting power. He is speciously attractive within, but only as a means of tempting and deceiving mankind.[12] His perversion of costuming convention in the play is thematically appropriate, for his resentment of God is directed against the very fact of mankind's likeness to the Godhead. "Of Gode man ys þe fygure," he laments, "Hys symylytude, hys pyctowre, / Gloryosest of ony creature / Þat euer was wrought" (ll. 349–52). It is the similitude that prompts Lucifer to seek to "dysvygure" this "Fygure of þe Godhede" through false conjecture (ll. 353–59). And it is because he recognizes the certainty of failure were he to "tempte man in my lyknes" that Lucifer resolves to "change me into bryghtnes" (ll. 373–75). His costume change at line 380 is thus one of manipulating appearances. He "dewoydyth and cummyth in ageyn as a goodly galont," delighting the audience with his skill in rapid theatrical change. The disguise of Lucifer as a proud gallant is like that in the N–Town Passion Play and like that of Pride (whose name as a gallant is "Curiosity") in the Digby *Mary Magdalene*.[13] He uses the contrast between outer and inner not as expressive of a spiritually divided nature, as in Anima, but as a device of illusion and convenience for rapid costume change. (The practical reason for having the gallant's costume on the inside, in fact,

WISDOM

is that it is easier and quicker for Lucifer to take off his outer devil's costume during his brief stay offstage than to put on a gallant's elaborate outfit.)[14] His alteration metadramatically calls attention to the theatrical nature of the trick to emphasize his skill as actor and playwright in his little drama of cunningly manipulated appearances. Mistrust of images, in the theater as in life, is a necessary condition of spiritual awareness.

Such a perception of falsity in images does not gainsay the moral dramatist's ability, nonetheless, to speak with unambiguous visual meaning. The alterations of Mind, Understanding, and Will form the center of the play's interest in costume change and bespeak a fall from grace to eventual recovery. The groups of retainers convey a similar point, of course, but in Mind, Understanding, and Will we see change adversely affecting the attributes of the soul itself. "Lewe yowr stodyes," Lucifer urges them, "Yowr prayers, yowr penance, of ipocryttys þe syne, / Ande lede a comun lyff"—that is, a life of ordinary sensual pleasures. "What synne ys in met, in ale, in wyn? / Wat synne ys in ryches, in clothynge fyne?" (ll. 470–74). The decisive stage action symbolizing such an embracement of the world is change of garb. "Change þat syde aray," urges Lucifer (l. 510), in reference to their long robes. We have seen them heretofore, in fact, dressed in "wyght cloth of golde" like Anima and the five wits, "cheveleryde" or wigged like her and "crestyde in sute," in the same dress (following l. 324). They have marched in liturgical procession with the five wits, and in every way their appearance has denoted their function as attributes of the soul. Now they "dyfye" their long garb and resolve to "be fresche" (ll. 510–11). They become the chief target of Lucifer's resolve to convert their "lyknes most amyable" to God into something "most reprouable" and "lyke to a fende of hell" (ll. 536–38). That does not mean, of course, that they appear as devils, for Lucifer himself is now dressed as a gallant. Instead, they return to the stage at line 551 "in a new aray," "fresche," "jolye," "lykynge" (ll. 551–67). Their delight in their "Fresche dysgysynge" (l. 590) suggests at once the literal meaning of newfangled dress and the theatrical meaning of disguise in a mumming or court entertainment. Their array is "curyous" (l. 609), that is, exquisite, and a good deal is made of its expense (l. 601). The elaborate costumes of their retainers merely express in larger configuration the costuming extravagances in which they indulge. It is through costume that Mind, Understanding, and Will reject the "Contemplatyff lyff" (l. 417) of their original clerical array for the garb of "þe worlde" (l. 442); they eschew "All syngler deuocyons" and their "stodyes" in favor of "precyus wede" that signifies "worschype" and "dominacyon" (ll. 452–70). Their interest in being fashionable prompts an interest in the "gyse of Frawnce" (l. 516). The indications are plentiful, then, that the corruption·of Mind, Understanding, and Will into Maintenance, Perjury, and Lechery is conveyed through sartorial signals of riotous excess and heavy expenditure.

Eventually, of course, Mind, Understanding, and Will are brought to their senses by Wisdom, and are taught to recognize their fall for what it is. "Se howe ye haue dysvyguryde yowr soule! / Beholde yowrselff; loke veryly in mynde!" (ll. 901–2). They have been so "onkynde as to "defoule Godys own place, /Þat was made so gloryus wythowt ende" (ll. 905–6). Their first step toward penance is literally that of being able to see their own disfigurement: "I se how I haue defowlyde þe noble kynde /Þat was lyke to þe by in-

Christ as "Eternal Wisdom." Heinrich Suso, from a manuscript of the German writings in the Herzog August Bibliothek. Wolffenbüttel (Codex Guelf, 78.5, Aug. Fol. 97R 1473.)

King Edward IV enthroned before William, Lord Herbert and his wife Anne. (John Lydgate, Troy Book. British Library Royal Ms. 18 D II, fol. 6)

King Edward IV, his queen and son, etc. From a small folio manuscript on vellum in the Archbishop's Library at Lambeth, no. 265.

King Henry VI and his parliament at Bury St. Edmund's, showing William Curteis, abbot of St. Edmundsbury Abbey presenting a book to the king. (Harleian Library MS 2278.)

Abbot Richard Hinghan and St. Edmund. Stained glass, now in north aisle of Church of the Holy Trinity, Long Melford, Suffolk. (Photo credit: G. M. Gibson.)

Trinity College Medieval Festival production of *Wisdom*, May 5, 1984. (Photo credit: Matthew Moore.)

The Ghent Altarpiece. Completed 1432. Hubert and Jan van Eyck. Middle upper register panels, Virgin, Christ Enthroned. Vijd Chapel, St. Bavo's Cathedral, Ghent.

tellygens," acknowledges Mind (ll. 927–28). They go with Anima to seek contrition and penance, and return once again in orderly procession, "all in here fyrst clothynge, her chapplettys and crestys, and all hauyng on crownys" (following l. 1064), singing a verse from the Psalms (115. 12, 13, King James Psalm 116) that has been associated with the Communion of the Mass since the ninth century.[15] Restoration of garment is the surest sign in the theater of restored graciousness in the eyes of God.

The central figure in this restoration is Anima herself. The acknowledgment by Mind, Understanding, and Will of their disfigurement is accompanied by the appearance of Anima "in þe most horrybull wyse, fowlere þan a fende" (following l. 902). Her dual nature, apparent from the start in her costume of inner white and outer black, yields now to grotesque images of utter foulness and to the forays of seven devils from beneath her "horrybyll mantyll." Her sole thought is of how she may regain her first appearance. "Why change I nowte, / I þat thus horryble in synne lye?" she cries. "What ys þat xall make me clene?" (ll. 950–54). Her contrition takes the form of stage gesture; she must "wepe for sorow" (l. 977), whereupon the seven black devils are expelled. She goes out singing "in þe most lamentabull wyse" (l. 996) and returns as she originally was, her soul "waschede" by Christ's passion in a "new resurreccyon" of God's grace (ll. 1069–71). She is, as Wisdom observes, "reformyde to yowr bewtys bryght" (l. 1092). Wisdom's last warning to her is never again to "Dysfygure yow" to "þe lyknes of þe fende" (l. 1114).

The visual structure of the play, then, places at its center the magisterial figure of Wisdom in regal purple and gold, and the dual, wavering image of the Soul.

One remains constant; the other makes a journey of fall and redemption that returns to its point of origin. All the visual contrasts of the play are extrapolations from this central configuration, elaborations in balanced symmetrical pairings that reinforce through juxtaposition the alternation of black and white, foul and fair. What I hope this illustrates, apart from a formal reading of the play itself, is the way in which morality drama gains its structure in good part by visualizing metaphor. Like the metaphors of soul-struggle, military conflict, or pilgrimage, the metaphor in this play of inner purity and outward corruption invites the dramatist to seek out costuming devices and groupings of characters through which to express the abstract teaching of his proposition. And it is this seeking out of lively theatrical embodiments for metaphor that gives to the morality drama its inventiveness, its imaginative effects, its comic routines, and above all its readily understood language of spiritual change and recovery.

NOTES

1. Walter Hilton, *Scala Perfectionis*, quoted in relevant parallel passages in Walter Kay Smart, *Some English and Latin Sources and Parallels for the Morality of Wisdom* (Menasha, Wis.: George Banta, 1912), pp. 18–22, and Mark Eccles, ed., *The Macro Plays*. Early English Text Society (London: Oxford University Press, 1969), p. 205. Textual quotations from *Wisdom* in this essay are based on Eccles's edition.

    Eugene Hill argues that in Augustinian terms Anima never loses the Trinitarian "image" of God; it is ob-

scured but never entirely effaced, whereas the "likeness" of God *is* defaced through the machinations of Lucifer. "The Trinitarian Allegory of the Moral Play of *Wisdom*," *Modern Philology*, 73 (1975): 121–35. Hilton's language, on the other hand, does describe the soul's fall from grace as one in which we see "nought but an ymage of the fende & a bronde of helle," suggesting that the word "image" can also be used to convey the sense of the soul's blackness. Hilton also speaks in a passage quoted in this essay of the "ymage of sinne," and the play of *Wisdom* picks this language up at line 140.
2. Smart, *Some English and Latin Sources*, p. 9.
3. David Bevington, *From "Mankind" to Marlowe* (Cambridge, Mass.: Harvard University Press, 1962), pp. 124–27.
4. Arnold Williams, "The English Moral Play before 1500," *Annuale Medievale* 4 (1963): 5–22, esp. p. 14.
5. A modern close translation of the Hebrew, *The New English Bible* (New York: Oxford University Press, 1971), renders these lines as follows: "I am dark but lovely, daughters of Jerusalem, / like the tents of Kedar / or the tent-curtains of Shalmah." This translation has also been used at footnote 7 and accompanying text.
6. Compare John Joseph Molloy, *A Theological Interpretation of the Moral Play*, "*Wisdom, Who Is Christ*" (Washington, D.C.: Catholic University of America Press, 1952), p. 30, who proposes that the five wits wear black mantles over their white robes.
7. Eccles, ed., *The Macro Plays*, p. 207.
8. Ibid., p. 212.
9. Molloy, *Theological Interpretation*, p. 115 n. 37.
10. Morton Bloomfield, *The Seven Deadly Sins* (East Lansing: Michigan State University Press, 1952; reprinted 1967), pp. 61–66.

11. David Bevington, *Tudor Drama and Politics* (Cambridge, Mass.: Harvard University Press, 1968), pp. 29–31.
12. Molloy, *Theological Interpretation*, p. 65.
13. Smart, *Some English and Latin Sources*, p. 46.
14. In *The Birth of Merlin* (1597–1621), the devil changes into a gallant in full sight of a clown figure who is also on stage; see Bevington, *From "Mankind" to Marlowe*, p. 94.
15. Molloy, *Theological Interpretation*, p. 157, citing William Durandus of Mende (d. 1276), *Rationale Divinorum Officiorum* (Venice, 1609), iv, 54, n. 10 seq.

The Play of *Wisdom* and the Abbey of St. Edmund

GAIL McMURRAY GIBSON

Piles of old stones have inspired English poets to create a venerable tradition of poems musing about the habitations and voices of the past. Medieval drama historians, too, are nudged to curiosity by the ruins and ciphers that hint at the past we want to know. Indeed, such clues point us at the lost coherence of a past we *must* know, for medieval theater in its time performed functions as immediate and practical, as grounded in human need, festival, and community as medieval Christendom itself. The registers of dialogue that survive can only speak when they are reunited with the spectacle that made them art and with the contractual purpose and context that made them exist at all. The drama historian's search for the coordinates of time and place, for dramatic provenance and motive, is neither empty academic exercise nor gossip, but is, I believe, central to the assumption that to know the medieval theater means to know it as fully as we can in its human particularity. This article begins with a play in search of a place, the fifteenth-century morality play called *Wisdom*—and with a pile of old stones.

These stones, these ruins must stand for a monastic house that for more than 500 years was one of the great cultural centers of England, where learned Benedictine monks copied manuscripts and wrote sermons and saints' lives, supervised their vast estates, quarreled with the grasping merchants and shopkeepers of their town, socialized with visiting prelates and princes, watched the pilgrims milling about in the monastery yard, and also, I believe, helped create one of the most diverse and important English dramatic traditions of the fifteenth century, a tradition that now lies hidden in a rubble of half-clues and riddles.[1] We must begin with the clues of the complete medieval copy of the play of *Wisdom*, a text in the collection of East Anglian plays we call the *Macro Plays* manuscript.

On folio 121 of that manuscript, at the end of the text of *Wisdom*, there is a single Latin inscription: "O liber si quis cui constas forte queretur/hynghamque monacho dices super omnia consto" (O book, if anyone shall perhaps ask to whom you belong, you will say, I belong above everything to Hyngham, a monk.)[2] As long ago as 1912, Walter Kay Smart suggested that this Hyngham was Richard Hengham or Hyngham, a Benedictine monk and Doctor of Canon Law who was abbot of Bury St. Edmunds from 1474 to 1479.[3] Although, as Richard Beadle cautions, any of the half dozen or so monk Hynghams who are known to have lived in East Anglia in the second half of the fifteenth century "might have been the Hingham of the *Macro Plays*,"[4] the likeliest candidate, as D. C. Baker and J. L. Murphy confirmed in an important article in *Research*

Opportunities in Renaissance Drama in 1967,[5] is Richard Hyngham of Bury.

For there is no doubt that the Macro manuscript has links with Bury St. Edmunds. There is the explicit evidence, first of all, of another inscription on fol. 105, in a later, perhaps early sixteenth-century hand, beginning "In the name of God amen I Rychard Cake of Bury . . . ." The second link to Bury St. Edmunds lies in the evidence or quite remarkable coincidence that the earliest recorded owners of the two manuscripts that contain texts of *Wisdom* were both natives of Bury St. Edmunds. The incomplete text of *Wisdom* that appears in the *Digby Plays* manuscript belonged to an alchemist, physician, and book collector named Myles Blomefylde, who was born in Bury in 1515, and the full *Wisdom* text of the *Macro Plays* manuscript first surfaced in the library of Cox Macro, an eighteenth-century manuscript collector who was son of Thomas Macro, five times the elected alderman of Bury St. Edmunds.[6] Cox Macro is known to have owned a number of manuscripts that had come from the monastery of Bury St. Edmunds, including the Great Register of the Abbey kept by Lydgate's abbot, William Curteys in the 1430s and 1440s.[7] It would appear, in other words, that in Monk Hyngham, in Richard Cake, in Myles Blomefylde, and in Cox Macro we have evidence for owners of manuscripts containing the play of *Wisdom* being at Bury St. Edmunds in the fifteenth, sixteenth, and eighteenth centuries.

There are a number of other names inscribed in the Macro manuscript besides monk Hyngham's and Richard Cake's; most of these are names appearing in contexts that suggest, as David Bevington observed in his edition of the Macro manuscript facsimile, schoolboy scribbles.[8] On the back of folio 121, for example, the name "Rainold Wodles" is spelled out in cipher code, each vowel being substituted for by the next letter of the alphabet (i.e., *b* for *a*, *f* for *e*, and so forth). Similar codes and cyphers are used throughout the manuscript for other names, and blank pages and spaces have been used for doodles, pen trials, and a remarkably unsuccessful attempt to translate a poem into Latin. One would feel safe in inferring that, between the time that Monk Hyngham wrote his name in the manuscript and the time that the manuscript shows up in Cox Macro's library, the text had been in several prankish, probably youthful, hands, either in a series of families or in a school of some kind. It may be relevant to the search for the Macro manuscript's history that there was a free grammar school at Bury and that both Thomas Macro and Cox Macro had close connections with it. Thomas Macro had been elected one of the governors of Bury School in 1689[9] and his son, Cox Macro, was a prominent benefactor of the school library.[10] It may also be significant that Bury School, although not established until the reign of Edward VI, seems to have been a direct descendant of the monastery's school for the sons of town burgesses; it was at least founded to compensate the town for the loss of the abbey school endowment which had been confiscated by the Crown along with other monastery property at the Dissolution.[11] We know little about the early library of this Bury School; it was only catalogued in 1672–1673 after it had moved to a new location on Northgate Street and after a committee had been appointed to decide "what books are fit to be continued in the Library, and what books are to be put out of the same."[12]

Whether or not Bury School is the link between the monastery library and Cox Macro's library, it is certain that the Macro manuscript contains numerous Bury names. The surname Plandon, for example, which appears in schoolboy cipher on folio 104 of the manuscript, is the name of a prominent Bury family.[13] The Robert Oliver, whose name appears both in signature and in cipher repeatedly in the manuscript, was perhaps a relative of the Bury physician Thomas Oliver who donated books to Bury School in 1595.[14] Richard Cake (fol. 105) calls himself "of Bury," but, whoever he was, he was not the sixteenth century "rector of Bradfield near Bury" as David Bevington and Mark Eccles have repeated from a double error in N.R. Ker's *Medieval Libraries of Great Britain*.[15] (Ker apparently conflated the names Richard Corke and Edmund Cake which appear consecutively in the Bradfield incumbents' list—but which is, anyway, not from one of the three Suffolk Bradfield parishes near Bury at all, but from Bradfield, Norfolk.)[16]

Whatever the *Macro Plays* connection with the sixteenth century Bury families whose names appear in the manuscript, we can assume, I think, that the *Macro Plays* were at the monastery of St. Edmund itself from the time of Abbot Hyngham in the late fifteenth century until the dissolution of the monastery in 1539. Now we know that manuscripts of the comedies of Plautus and Terence were by the twelfth century in the library of Bury St. Edmunds abbey but that does not prove that they were performed there. (Although, interestingly enough, the 1550 Statutes of Bury School specify that the third form students were to study the "chaster plays of Plautus and Terence" and that a play was to be performed by the school every year at the end of winter term.)[17] What does it mean to say that a manuscript in which the play of *Wisdom* appears came from the monastery of St.

Edmund? Or more to the point, what evidence is there that Bury St. Edmunds had an active tradition of performing drama rather than just a monk Hyngham interested in collecting play texts?

First of all, it is important to note that both the Digby and the Macro texts of *Wisdom* are acting texts—or at least the records of an actual performance. As Donald Baker has observed in his edition of the fragmentary Digby text of *Wisdom*, both the Macro and Digby texts of *Wisdom* record marginal notes indicating that the lines containing the masked dances of three Mights' retainers were to be omitted.[18] And not only was this early sixteenth-century scribe of the Digby play text apparently still interested in copying the performance notes of a fifteenth-century play text (perhaps a unique occasion in the history of English theater), but manuscript evidence argues that the abbey's dramatic tradition goes back even 100 years before the *Macro Plays*. The fourteenth-century drama fragment known as the *Rickinghall Fragment* was written in Anglo-Norman on the backs of pages recording the abbey's manorial accounts from the Suffolk manor of Rickinghall, an estate belonging to the Bury St. Edmunds monastery until the confiscation of monastic lands by Henry VIII.[19].

The archival evidence of actual dramatic performance at Bury St. Edmunds is, however, both as fragmented and as tantalizing as the rubble of the abbey itself. A guild certificate return of 1389 tersely lists among the functions of the Corpus Christi guild of St. James Church of Bury that of providing an "interludium" of Corpus Christi.[20] The Weavers' Guild Ordinance of 1477 decrees that half of fines for craft guild violations go to the sacristan of the abbey (who had titular control of all trade in the borough of the town) and that the other half go toward the expenses of a pageant of the Ascension and Pentecost "as yt hath be customed of olde tyme owte of minde yeerly to be had to the wurschepe of God, amongge other payenttes in the processione in the feste of Corpus Xti."[21] Neither one of these references tells us any more than the fact that dramatic spectacle was observed in the town and that drama, like everything else in Bury St. Edmunds, was linked to the powerful Benedictine abbey here. Indeed, the very parish church of St. James in which the Corpus Christi guild worshipped was under the rectorship of the monastery and was even built within the monastery grounds.

Bury St. Edmunds was one of the most notable examples in medieval England of a monastic borough; the abbot of St Edmund was not only spiritual lord of an important monastic center, he was both spiritual and temporal lord of the town. The abbey in fact had a virtual monopoly over every conceivable activity of the town of Bury. It controlled the marketplace and town tournaments; it was landlord of all property in the borough and immediate suburbs; it had its own court where it heard legal cases and probated and registered wills; it was responsible for the town jail, minted coins, and had the rights to everything from street manure for the abbey's vineyards and fields to the appointing of parish priests and chaplains to lead the spiritual life of every man, woman, and child in the town.[22] In short, the monastery was directly or indirectly involved in every aspect of civic life in Bury St. Edmunds. It should hardly be surprising that fifteenth-century life in the monastery of St. Edmund seems to have been marked by a vested interest in the court politics and cloth trade and successful harvests of the world outside its walls. It should hardly be surprising that the plays in

Monk Hyngham's manuscript show us such a broad and generous understanding of the seductions of the lay world, for, at Bury as elsewhere in the fifteenth century, the monastic life and the teeming life of the town had literally met each other halfway.

Let us accept, then, that there are drama texts linked with the monastery of St. Edmund, and let us accept that there was religious drama performed at Bury under its aegis, even though we know little about that drama except that it existed. If it is as John Wasson called it in his edition of the Suffolk dramatic records "an under-exposed picture," it is nonetheless a suggestive one.[23] Suggestive all the more when we consider that it is sheer chance that any records at all survive from the monastery of Bury. When the monastery property was confiscated by the Crown in 1539, the very lead was stripped from the roof of the magnificent abbey church, the stones of the monastery buildings broken up and sold by the cartload for building material, and most of the 2,000 manuscripts of the library and the 500 or more years of record-keeping scattered, destroyed, or lost. Only a handful of documents remain, for example, to hint at the entire last century of the abbey's existence. Yet even these documents—sacrist registers of 1418, of 1429–30, of 1537, and the two years of late medieval feretrar's or shrine-keepers' accounts (1520–21) that survived because they had been deposited for some reason in the town guildhall chest—can tell us something about the rich festival life of the great abbey. These documents can tell us, for example, that the monastery made annual donations to the Boy Bishop festivities (sponsored jointly with the town confraternity called Dusse guild); these payments "in honorem sancti Nicholai" appear until 1537.[24] These accounts also tell us that the abbey paid for minstrels at Christmas and at the feast of its patron, St. Edmund, on November 20th (noted in 1418 and 1429–30.)[25] In 1520 the feretrars' account roll listed expenses for singers in the chapel of St. Robert of Bury,[26] a local child saint believed to have been martyred by the Jews. In the mere six years of relevant account records that survive from the fifteenth and early sixteenth centuries, there are also numerous references to the abbey's payments to unspecified minstrels, "players," and mimes as well as to minstrels and mimes of the king (these "regis nimis" were paid during the reigns of Henry VII and Henry VIII), and to minstrels of the Count of Oxford, the Lord of Arundel, the Earl of Darby, the Duke of Norfolk, and the Duke of Somerset.[27] It was the prior who ordered the entertainments in most cases, and there is a payment in 1506 to "ludentibus in aula et camera prioris" (to players in the hall and chamber of the prior).[28] The prior is also mentioned in one of the most intriguing of the payments listed in the 1520 feretrar's accounts: "To men who came with a camel, by the prior's order 1 d."[29]

None of these surviving records are from the 1460s, the likely date of the *Wisdom* play in the Macro manuscript, and none of these records offer any elaboration about the kinds of dramatic and musical entertainments presented in the chambers of the monastery. We can therefore neither prove that the play of *Wisdom* was or was not performed at Bury, although we can say with certainty that the monastery of St. Edmund was the site of dramatic festivities both liturgical and worldly and that our best evidence suggests that the *Macro Plays* anthology of dramatic texts comes from that monastery. What the text of *Wisdom* also demonstrates clearly is that the play both directs itself to lay members of its audience as well as dramatizes a specifically monastic sin—the temptation to abandon the contemplative life. Lucifer's temptation is simple and explicit: "Go in þe worlde, se þat abowte."[30] I shall summarize as tactfully as possible by saying simply that the Benedictine monastery of Bury St. Edmunds is an entirely possible setting and provenance for the play.[31] We should turn, now, to the monastery of Bury itself as we try to visualize the place and the audience much like—if not indeed synonymous with—that which viewed the pageant of *Wisdom*.

The Benedictine abbey of Bury St. Edmunds, dedicated to Christ, the Virgin Mary, and to St. Edmund—an East Anglian king murdered by the Vikings in the ninth century—was one of the five richest monasteries in medieval England. By the end of the fifteenth century, it normally housed between seventy and eighty monks; David Knowles suggests that by 1500 probably only Canterbury had a larger population.[32] The monastery walls enclosed forty acres, but the abbey through a combination of royal grants and favors and pious bequests had amassed by the end of the fifteenth century most of the estates and church tithes in southwest Suffolk. The abbot, prior, and sacrist were the chief officers of what was by the fifteenth century an immensely wealthy household corporation. In addition to the seventy or eighty monks at Bury, there were fifteen chaplains who attended the abbot and chief officers, and about forty members of the secular clergy who were appointed by the abbot to officiate in the churches and guild and hospital chapels in the town and to teach in the abbey schools. There were apparently three schools at Bury—a school for noviciates near the monastery cloister, a song school to prepare boys for the secular clergy, and a free school for the sons of prominent Bury burgesses.[33] A monastery document from the second half of the 13th century tells us that in the time of Edward I there were also 111 common servants housed at the abbey;[34] by the late Middle Ages, this number was probably closer to 200.

The abbot of Bury exercised absolute authority, spiritual and temporal, within the Liberty of St. Edmund—in the entire town and suburbs of the town for one mile in every direction as well as in the monastery itself. Because of his temporal authority within the Liberty, the abbot of Bury sat in Parliament, bore the title of lord, and like other great provincial lords maintained a London palace (at "Bevis Marks," originally "Bury Marks" beside Christ Church, Aldgate).[35] A rich and pious Bury cloth merchant named John Baret, who seems to have been a personal friend or patron of the poet Lydgate, left a will in 1468 in which he refers to himself as "a gentleman of my lord abbot's household" and in which he leaves a series of personal remembrances to the chief officers of the abbey and to their yeomen, grooms, and pages as well as general alms gifts to the entire convent. Baret's will also leaves a purse of silk and gold to "every gentylman of my lord abbotte which be comyng and goyng as officeres and menyal men longyng to the houshold of my felashippe,"[36] a bequest that confirms that the abbot of Bury's palace was much like the court of a king or a great lord, a place bustling with civil servants, functionaries, and courtiers. It is not Benedict's *Rule*, then, that should be in our minds as we envision the fifteenth-century monastery of Bury St. Edmunds, but the household of great East Anglian magnates like the Dukes of Norfolk.

Unlike such great provincial lords, however, the abbot of Bury claimed a charter of privileges that made the abbey exempt from all other jurisdiction except that of the king and the pope—a claim that frequently led to friction with the Bishop of Norwich and even more frequently to friction in the town of Bury.[37] The monastery's unceasing diligence in maintaining control of the borough raised increasing resentment as the town flourished in the cloth trade, and the conflict was at its heart an economic one. The town and the abbey were locked into economic conflict for several centuries because the town wanted to reap the economic and social advantages of the monastery and of the pilgrims and trade it brought to the town, but without owing economic obligations to it. In the fourteenth-century, the town's dissent once erupted into open violence in which the monastery was ransacked and the prior murdered, but the heavy penalties exacted by the king as punishment resigned the town to more peaceable forms of protest. In the late fifteenth-century, for example, Jankyn Smith of Bury was to ensure his legend as town benefactor forever (his death day is still commemorated in an annual civic ceremony in Bury St. Edmunds) by bequeathing his considerable land holdings to be held in trust by the town to pay the hated "Abbot's Cope," the 100 marks tax demanded of the citizens at each new installation of a new abbot.[38]

That determined overlord, the monastery of St. Edmund, was a formidable physical fact as well as authority in the town. Printed here is W. K. Hardy's useful 1883 reconstruction of the appearance of the abbey shortly before the Reformation, "chiefly from existing remains," according to the artist's inscription. What even such a hypothetical reconstruction can show is the looming physical presence of the pilgrimage church of St. Edmund, 505 feet long (and fifty feet longer than Norwich Cathedral). The great monastery wall enclosing the abbey was linked to the town by the two, still surviving, fifteenth-century churches of St. James (slightly to the left of the abbey church) and St. Mary of the Assumption (at the far right-hand corner), built by the abbey to serve as parish churches for the town. Directly adjacent to the north side of the abbey church were the main convent buildings: the chapter house, library and novice's school, the refectory, and the cloister where the monks who were not off managing estates or studying at Oxford or Cambridge, or in residence at the abbot's London palace would have sat at their desks reading, writing, or copying manuscripts. To the left of the cloister was the Great Court; at the far north side were a wide range of buildings and offices necessary to the maintenance of this huge, wealthy community—including a bakery, stables, and grain storehouse. The entire east side was a complex of residential buildings known as the Abbot's Palace. It would have been here that eminent guests to the monastery would have been quartered, feasted, and entertained. The main part of the Abbot's Palace had been built in the latter part of the thirteenth century when King Henry III had visited the abbey several times, but when, in 1433, Abbot Curteys received eight weeks notice that King Henry VI was coming to spend Christmas at the abbey, he set eighty men to work, day and night, improving, repairing, and rebuilding his palace.[39]

The main public room of the Abbot's Palace was the abbot's dining hall. Archaeological evidence suggests that the hall was about fifty-five feet long and forty-eight feet wide. It was built over a lower floor room known as the abbot's parlor, constructed with five-foot thick walls, and supported by ten massive pillars in an octagon arrangement. At the northwest corner was a turret or tower, designed to give an overlook over the courtyard. Just behind the Abbot's Palace was an enclosed garden, an acre in size, that was also apparently the site of the building where the abbey minted its own coins.[40] The prior also had elegant chambers and his own hall. During Henry VI's visit to the abbey, the king moved to the prior's chambers so, we are told, he would have readier access to the hunting fields behind the abbey; the prior's lodging subsequently came to be called King's Hall.[41] Unlike the rest of the monastic buildings, which were stripped of all valuables at the Reformation, then carted away, stone by stone, as building material, the Abbot's Palace remained intact and was occupied as a private residence until 1720.[42] A second black-and-white sketch shows the Abbot's Palace as it looked about 1680, from the west, with (above) a view of the south side of the great court. When the Abbot's Palace was pulled down in 1720, the only surviving interior remains of the abbey complex was the ruined west front of the abbey church. Those ruins had by now become fashionably picturesque, and several eighteenth-century town houses and shops were built into the remains.

We can get a better idea of the splendor of the abbey's Great Court and the Abbot's Palace from the surviving outer entrance gate, the Great Gate that abuts upon the marketplace street now called Angel Hill. The Great Gate was erected in 1347 to replace a gate destroyed in the 1327 riot (described above). It was no doubt with those shocking events in mind that this new gate was constructed with an upper guard room and arrow slits and archers' stations located behind the statuary niches.[43] Royal support of the abbey, however, was strong enough so that the town in the

Drawing by Edmund Prideaux of the abbot's palace around 1680 from the west (below) and from the south side (above) of the Great Court of the Monastery. Reproduced by permission of Mr. J. C. F. Prideaux-Brune. (Photo: National Monuments Record.)

W. K. Hardy, "The Monastery of the Bury St. Edmunds before the Dissolution, conjectural restoration, chiefly from existing remains" (1883). From the *St. Edmundsbury Borough Guide* with the permission of the editor, Councillor H. R. Marsh. (Photo: O.G. Jarman.)

fifteenth century, but for occasional disputes in the courts, seems to have resigned itself to the abbot's rule.

The ultimate source of the abbey's power and of its prestige was the shrine of St. Edmund, whose body had been brought to Bury, then called Bedericsworth, in 903. The body of the saint was enclosed by a magnificent gold and jewel-crusted sepulchre behind the high altar, so laden with treasures and with the votive offerings of centuries of pilgrims that at the Reformation Henry VIII's commissioners complained that it was "very cumbersome to deface."[44] The legend of Edmund says that he was tied to a tree and shot with arrows, then decapitated, because he refused to share his Christian kingdom with the Viking invaders who had overrun Suffolk and Norfolk in the year 869. The abbey tradition of involvement in political affairs thus begins as early as the martyrdom of Edmund himself. For Bury St. Edmunds was not only vitally important as a center of learning and culture—it had one of the greatest manuscript scriptoria of the fourteenth and fifteenth centuries and was the home of the most important poet of the fifteenth century, the monk John Lydgate—it was never far removed from the high politics of the times. It was before the altar of the abbey church at Bury St. Edmunds, for example, that English barons first met in the thirteenth century to swear to an alliance that would force King John to capitulate to the demands we now know as the Magna Carta. Indeed, when Bury was finally incorporated as a town, not until the reign of James I, it was granted a crest with the motto "Sacrarium Regis, Cunabula Legis" (Shrine of a King, Cradle of the Law).[45]

Bury St. Edmunds was hardly ever more involved with royal politics than it was in the fifteenth century when Abbot Curteys developed a close, even fatherly, relationship to the child king, Henry VI. As a boy of twelve, Henry VI spent the months from Christmas 1433 to Easter 1434 as a houseguest at the monastery of Bury, an unusually lengthy visit that was recognized as an extraordinary sign of the king's favor. At the end of this famous visit came a solemn ceremony in the chapter house in which the king and his courtiers were admitted to lay confraternity status in the abbey of St. Edmund.[46] The role of Bury St. Edmund's abbey as special supporter of King Henry VI was underlined by the meeting of Parliament in 1447 in the refectory of the monastery to try the case of Humphrey, Duke of Gloucester for plotting against the king, who by that time was exhibiting the bizarre and distracted, perhaps feeble-minded, behavior that caused his followers to hail him as a saint and his detractors to mock him as a madman.[47] John Lydgate, monk of Bury, waged a one-man propaganda campaign for the king and the Lancastrian dynasty, writing political poems in which Henry is extravagantly praised and extolled as both king of England and rightful king of France. After Henry's 1433 visit, Abbot Curteys commissioned from Lydgate a verse account of the life and miracles of St. Edmund and had it splendidly illuminated. Lydgate's *Life of St. Edmund* was presented to King Henry VI, says Lydgate's poem, in hope and expectation that Henry would be the embodiment of the ideal Christian king, the guardian and defender of the Church—and especially the guardian of the church of St. Edmund.[48] We know that Henry VI was repeatedly a visitor to the abbey of Bury St. Edmunds; there are records of visits in 1436, 1446 and 1448[49] in addition to the long Christmas visit of 1433. Indeed, even after

Henry's apparent complete mental breakdown in 1453, the monastery of St. Edmund continued to be one of the king's chief defenders.

The monastery was also involved in the political affairs of Henry VI's ambitious French queen, Margaret of Anjou, and that support began even before her coronation. A letter survives in the fifteenth-century register of Abbot Curteys in which Henry VI had appealed to his old friend Abbot Curteys for a loan to help finance the royal pageantry deemed necessary to bring Margaret to London "in suche wise as it shall be according to the state and worshipe of us, of hir, and of this oure reaume, and, that doone, to purveye for the solemnite of hir coronation in maner and fourme accustumed."[50] The Bury monk and poet John Lydgate, who had supervised Henry VI's pageants in Paris, was traditionally credited with writing the speeches for the pageants welcoming Margaret to London; a recent article by Gordon Kipling challenges that ascription,[51] but does not challenge, I think, the real truth of the tradition—that both the names of Lydgate and Bury were automatically associated with acts of public support for the Lancastrian dynasty.

Thus it is hardly surprising that within a year of the Yorkist king Edward IV's seizing of the English throne, a concerted effort was made to root out the strong Lancastrian support centered in the Bury area. In 1462, six influential Suffolk noblemen and merchants were arrested for treasonous conspiracy with Margaret of Anjou and were charged with plotting to restore her young son as monarch. It is significant that not only were all six of those Suffolk leaders staunch patrons of Bury abbey, but that several of them had actually been admitted to lay brotherhood status there. All of those charged were executed at the Tower of London in

1462 except for John Clopton, a lay brother of the abbey and wealthy cloth merchant from the Suffolk village of Long Melford where the abbots of Bury had a country estate.[52] Clopton, the survivor, returned home to finance the rebuilding of the spectacular parish church at Long Melford in which his stained glass portrait still survives, conspicuously decorated with Edward IV's Yorkist white roses.[53]

Similar hasty political realignment was necessary at the abbey itself. In the same year that Edward IV executed the Suffolk Lancastrian leaders, he charged the abbot and entire convent at Bury with suspected treason and ordered the monastery placed under surveillance, supposedly for posting a notice on the abbey church door stating that the Pope had given "plenary absolution to all adherents of Henry VI, and had excommunicated all Edward's adherents."[54] After the abbot had been forced to pay the king the huge fine of 500 marks, the abbey managed to obtain a general pardon, and despite this inauspicious beginning, Edward IV and the monastery of Bury St. Edmunds seem to have reached a mutual understanding—or at least a truce. It is emblematic of the abbey's abrupt change in politics that Lydgate's propaganda poem, "Ab inimicis, or A Prayer for King, Queen, and People," written for Henry VI and his mother Catherine at the time of the coronation in 1429, appears in a later fifteenth-century version in several East Anglian manuscripts with the dedication and the praise altered to Edward IV.[55] Likewise, one of the surviving manuscript copies of Lydgate's *Life of St. Edmund* carefully suppresses all the references to Henry VI and to the Bury visit that was the occasion for the poem, while extending to a new monarchy the old poem's message that "royal power must yield before the virtue of humility and the omnipotence of God."[56] This is precisely the message of a play like *Wisdom*, and here we must return to the play in the Macro manuscript and to its possible historical context.

The date of the play of *Wisdom* was almost certainly the 1460s; the text can be dated both because of internal textual evidence and because of the argument that Monk Hyngham, if he was indeed Richard Hyngham, would have probably identified himself as Abbot Hyngham by 1474. Milla Riggio, in her splendid production of the play at Trinity College in 1984, hypothesized that the kingship masque of Wisdom might well have been a presentation before an actual monarch and presented the play as if it were a performance at Bury St. Edmunds before King Edward IV in 1474. That hypothesis created a dramatic truth that taught the spectators to see that the play was about kingship under the perspective of eternity, and it may have had a certain historical truth as well. It is entirely possible, in fact, that Edward IV could have seen the play of *Wisdom* at Bury, not in 1474, but in 1469. It was in 1469 that Edward IV traveled to Bury St. Edmunds for the first (and, as far as I have been able to determine), only time, although he was in the 1480s in frequent communication with the abbey through the royal councillors he dispatched to investigate a legal dispute between the monastery and the town burgesses.[57] We not only know that King Edward IV was at Bury in 1469, we know, too, that he came there on a pilgrimage to honor the shrine of King Edmund.[58] From Bury, Edward went to the famous pilgrimage shrine at Walsingham in Norfolk—and then he went to war. Many historians, in fact, see the Bury and Walsingham pilgimages as thinly disguised "recruiting tours"[59] since they turned out to be the preamble to Edward's northern military campaign. It is, however, doubtful that Edward IV was aware on that trip to Bury in June, 1469 that the next twenty-three months would be, as the historian Charles Ross has described it, "a period of political instability without parallel in English history since 1066."[60] For instead of returning, as announced, to London after the Bury-Walsingham pilgrimages, Edward IV wrote from Norwich for supplies and armor and headed toward the north with his entourage with the aim of helping his armies put down what he thought was a minor revolt of northern rebels. The insurrection, supposedly led by a champion of the poor who called himself "Robin of Redesdale," turned out to be a careful plot engineered by Edward's dangerous rival, the Earl of Warwick. In July, 1469, Edward's ill-prepared army was defeated and several of Edward's closest friends and advisers killed. By the next year, 1470, Edward had been forced to flee the country and the Earl of Warwick had placed the now totally lunatic king, Henry VI, back on the English throne, a puppet for Warwick's own political machinations. In 1471 Edward would return to England, overthrow both Warwick and the indefatigable Margaret of Anjou and recover the throne. Control of the government of England, in other words, changed hands completely three times in the twelve months immediately following Edward's visit to Bury St. Edmunds.[61]

In the final and decisive battle at Tewkesbury in April, 1471, both Margaret's seventeen-year old son and her hopes would die, and Henry VI would die soon after, of shock according to his contemporary chroniclers, more likely by Edward's order.[62] There is little wonder that fifteenth-century texts seem obsessed with the wheel of fortune and the mutability of man—or that a play like *Wisdom* would contrast the chaos and turbulence of worldly kingdoms with the serenity of the enthroned, contemplative Wisdom who is Christ. No records remain to tell us what happened when King Edward IV was at Bury in 1469 or how he was entertained or what Monk Hyngham and the other monks of Bury thought of the political chaos raging within and without their abbey walls or about their new, uneasy relationship to the Yorkist monarch. There is no proof that the play in the Macro manuscript, whose central image is a crowned king, was performed before the entourage of Edward IV. What I have tried to suggest is a likely context and a likely place from the fragments of stone and history that are now the play's only setting. What we do know is that it was in the very year of Edward's visit to Bury, in 1469, that King Edward IV issued a royal decree reconfirming the abbot of Bury's charter of privileges and ordering that the abbot's exclusive jurisdiction in the town be strictly observed, and that no secular officer should even enter the borough "except by consent of the abbot and convent."[63]

Given Edward's hostile actions against the abbey just eight years before, this reconfirmation of the Liberty of St. Edmund must be taken as remarkable evidence of royal favor—and of political regrouping. It is no exaggeration to say that Edward IV's support of the abbot's claims had the practical effect of bestowing royal benediction on the abbey of a kind that was to be every bit as influential as the long-standing Lancastrian support the abbey had enjoyed. It may be that the play of *Wisdom* was the abbey's gift in return. The loving reconciliation of Anima and the crowned king of Wisdom could have been intended as compliment to the king whose royalty was figured in the play, as well as a moral lesson, and as a resonant symbol of concord. For it was King Edward who had finally come to Bury in a conspicuous gesture of reverence for the shrine of St. Edmund, Edward who was now proclaiming himself, like Wisdom, the "Spows of þe chyrche and wery patrone."[64]

NOTES

1. On Bury St. Edmunds as a dramatic center, see W. A. Davenport, *Fifteenth-Century English Drama: The Early Plays and their Literary Relations* (Cambridge: D.S. Brewer, 1982), pp. 132–137; Gail McMurray Gibson, "Bury St. Edmunds, Lydgate, and the *N-Town Cycle*," *Speculum* 56 (1981), 56–90; and my forthcoming book-length study of East Anglian art, drama, and spirituality.
2. See the facsimile edition of *Wisdom* edited by David Bevington (*The Macro Plays* [Washington, D.C.: The Folger Shakespeare Library, 1972], pp. 248–249). The same inscription appears at folio 134 at the end of the play of *Mankind*. Bevington (p. 248) describes these inscriptions as being in "a different hand" from the main texts of the manuscript, but, in a recent article in *ELN* entitled "The Scribal Problem in the Macro Manuscript," Richard Beadle presents detailed paleographical argument that "Hyngham himself, or someone who wrote very similarly, is likely to have been the W-M scribe," *English Language Notes*, XXI, no. 4 (June, 1984), 9.
3. Walter Kay Smart, *Some English and Latin Sources and Parallels for the Morality of Wisdom* (Menasha, Wisconsin: George Banta, 1912), p. 86.
4. Beadle, "The Scribal ... Problem," p. 12.
5. D.C. Baker and J.L. Murphy, "The Late Medieval Plays

of Ms. Digby 133: Scribes, Dates and Early History, *Research Opportunities in Renaissance Drama* 10 (1967),.

6. See Baker and Murphy, "Late Medieval Plays," pp. 163–164 and Gibson, "Bury St. Edmunds, *Lydgate, and N-Town Cycle*," pp. 62–63.

7. Samuel Tymms, "Little Haugh Hall, Norton" [the home of the Macro family], *Suffolk Institute of Archaeology, Statistics, and Natural History Proceedings* 2 (1859), 284.

8. Bevington, *Macro Plays*, p. xix, observes that many of the sixteenth-century inscriptions in the manuscript "take on a playful turn, as though prankish scribes or young scholars were devising messages and even indecencies to one another under the cover of a secret code."

9. Tymms, "Little Haugh Hall," p. 281.

10. A.T. Bartholomew and Cosmo Gordon, "On the Library at King Edward VI School, Bury St. Edmunds," *The Library*, 3rd series, 1, i (1910), 8.

11. On the history of the Bury St. Edmunds Grammar School, see *The Victoria History of the County of Suffolk*, ed., William Page (London: Archibald Constable and Company, 1907), II, 306–318.

12. Bartholomew and Gordon, "On the Library," p. 9.

13. Bury and West Suffolk Record Office, Prob. Reg. Pye, fol. 17. Another John Plandon is named in a Bury will of 1504. See Samuel Tymms, ed., *Wills and Inventories from the Registers of the Commissary of Bury St. Edmunds and the Archdeacon of Sudbury*, Camden Society 49 (London: Camden Society, 1850), 98.

14. Bartholomew and Gordon, "On the Library." p. 2.

15. N.R. Ker, *Medieval Libraries of Great Britain*, 2nd ed., (London: Offices of the Royal Historical Society, 1964), p. 286. Cf. Mark Eccles, ed., *The Macro Plays*, EETS o.s. 262 (London: Oxford University Press,

1969), p. xxix, and Bevington, *Macro Plays*, p. viii.
16. A list of the incumbents of Bradfield, Norfolk, near Norwich appears in volume II of the *Notes of Bishop Thomas Tanner (1674–1735), Bury and West Suffolk Record Office microfilm J510/2 (Acc. 1230).*
17. *Victoria History of the County of Suffolk*, II, 314, 318. On the Bury mss. of Plautus and Terence, see R.M. Thomson, "The Library of Bury St. Edmunds Abbey in the Eleventh and Twelfth Centuries," *Speculum* 47 (1972), 633.
18. Donald C. Baker, John L. Murphy, and Louis B. Hall, Jr., eds., *The Late Medieval Religious Plays of Bodleian Mss. Digby 133 and E. Museo 160*, EETS o.s. 283 (London: Oxford University Press, 1982), p. lxxi.
19. See Norman Davis, ed., *Non-Cycle Plays and Fragments*, EETS s.s. 1 (London: Oxford University Press, 1970), pp. cxiv–cxv.
20. Public Record Office C. 47/46/401. For text see Alan H. Nelson, *The Medieval English Stage* (Chicago: University of Chicago Press, 1974), p. 189, and Karl Young, "An Interludium for a Gild of Corpus Christi," *Modern Language Notes* 48 (1933), 85–86.
21. Bury and West Suffolk Record Office B9/1/2. See William Dunn Macray, ed., *The Manuscripts of Lincoln, Bury St. Edmunds and Great Grimsby Corporations and of the Deans and Chapters of Worcester and Lichfield, Fourteenth Report, Part 8*, Historical Manuscripts Commission of Great Britain 65 (London, 1895), pp. 134–136; E.K. Chambers, *The Mediaeval Stage* (Oxford, 1903), II, 343–344. A reference to the Bury "pageants," appears at the foot of a 1558 note of rents from the Bury Guildhall. See Gibson, "Bury St. Edmunds, Lydgate, and N-Town Cycle," p. 61.
22. For the role of the abbey in the affairs of the town see M.D. Lobel, *The Borough of Bury St. Edmunds: A Study in the Government and Development of a Me-*

dieval Town (Oxford: Oxford University Press, 1935) and Robert S. Gottfried, *Bury St. Edmunds and the Urban Crisis: 1290–1539* (Princeton, N.J.: Princeton University Press, 1982).

23. David Galloway and John Wasson, *Records of Plays and Players in Norfolk and Suffolk, 1330–1642*, Malone Society Collections XI (Oxford: Oxford University Press, 1980–81), p. 147.

24. See Macray, *The Manuscripts of Lincoln, Bury St. Edmunds*, pp. 123-125.

25. Ibid., pp. 124–125.

26. Now Bury and West Suffolk Record Office A6/1/17. For the shrinekeepers' reference to singers in St. Robert's Chapel (and for several other references to minstrels, entertainments, and players not listed in the Malone Society *Records of Plays and Players in Norfolk and Suffolk*), see Macray, Manuscripts of Lincoln, Bury St. Edmunds, pp. 157–158.

27. See Macray, *Manuscripts of Lincoln, Bury St. Edmunds*, pp. 123–125, 157–158, and Galloway and Wasson, *Records of Plays*, pp. 147–148.

28. Galloway and Wasson, p. 148.

29. Macray, p. 157.

30. Eccles, ed., *The Macro Plays*, p. 130 (1. 501).

31. In an article entitled "Mysticism and Satire in the Morality of Wisdom" (*Philogical Quarterly* 53 [1974], 342–362), Milton McC. Gatch argues for *Wisdom*'s provenance at the London palace of the Bishop of Ely in Holburn, near the Inns of Court. His main arguments are a reference to Ely's patroness, St. Etheldreda ("Sent Audre"), in line 832 of the play and what he sees as the emphasis in the play's satire "on evils traditionally associated with the private lives of lawyers and other hangers-on of the law courts" (p. 358). Gatch, acknowledging the play's manuscript connections with Bury St. Edmunds, suggests that "it is

conceivable that a monk of Bury (which is geographically proximate to Ely and had close relations with Ely in the fifteenth century) in the service of the bishop of Ely or lodging in Ely Palace wrote the play or copied it to bring back to the monastery" (p. 361, n. 62). Such an hypothesis is given some substantiation, perhaps, by Donald Baker's argument (see Baker, et al., *The Late Medieval Religious Plays*, p. lxvi) that both the Macro and the Digby texts of *Wisdom*, "were copied from a common exemplar." Whether the play's original sponsor was the Benedictine monastery of Ely before it was copied for the Benedictine monastery of Bury seems entirely possible—but not possible to prove from a single reference to a popular East Anglian saint or from a general catalogue of London legal abuses. The abbot of Bury, it should be noted, also had a London town house as well as a steady stream of London pilgrims and dignitaries at Bury, and Richard Hyngham was a doctor of canon law.

32. Dom David Knowles, *The Religious Orders in England* (Cambridge: Cambridge University Press, 1979), II, p. 258.
33. Claude Messent, *The Monastic Remains of Norfolk and Suffolk* (Norwich: H.W. Hunt, 1934), p. 115.
34. Ibid.
35. Samuel Tymms, *A Handbook of Bury St. Edmunds* (Bury St. Edmunds, 1854), pp. 4–5.
36. Tymms, *Wills and Inventories*, p.16. On John Baret of Bury, see also Gibson, "Bury St. Edmunds, Lydgate, and the *N-Town Cycle*," pp. 72–73 and Gail McMurray Gibson, "East Anglian Drama and the Dance of Death: Some Second Thoughts on the 'Dance of Paul's'" *Early Drama, Art, and Music Newsletter* 5 no. 1 (1982): 1–9.
37. On the struggles between the abbey and the "burghal elite" of Bury St. Edmunds, see Gottfried, pp. 215–236. Cf. Gottfried, p. 215: "The dominant fact of political

WISDOM

life in the late medieval Bury St. Edmunds was that the Benedictine abbey ran the town; the dominant activity was the struggle of the town's burghal élite to assert their independence."

38. See Margaret Statham, "The Guildhall, Bury St. Edmunds." *Proceedings of the Suffolk Institute of Archeology and History* 31 (1968), pp. 140–141.
39. A.B. Whittingham, *Bury St. Edmunds Abbey, Suffolk* (London: H.M.S.O., 1976), pp. 8–9.
40. See Tymms, *Handbook*, pp. 9–10 and A.B. Whittingham, "Bury St. Edmunds Abbey: The Plan, Design, and Development of the Church and Monastic Buildings," *Archaeological Journal* 108 (1951), p. 184.
41. Sir William Dugdale, *Monasticon Anglicanum* (London: James Bohn, 1846), III, 113.
42. Whittingham, *Bury St. Edmunds Abbey, Suffolk*, p.12.
43. Whittingham, "Bury St. Edmunds Abbey: The Plan," p. 186.
44. G.H. Cook, ed., *Letters to Cromwell and Others on the Suppression of the Monasteries* (London, 1965), p. 114.
45. H. Marcus Bird, "The Story of Bury St. Edmunds," in *Borough of St. Edmundsbury*, ed., Harry R. Marsh (Norwich: Jarrold and Sons, Ltd., 1976), p. 18.
46. Dugdale, *Monasticon*, III, 113. For an account of Henry VI's visit, see also Walter Schirmer, *John Lydgate, A Study in the Culture of the XVth Century*, trans. Ann E. Keep (London: Methuen and Company, 1961), pp. 144–146.
47. E.F. Jacob, *The Fifteenth Century* (Oxford: Oxford University Press, 1960), pp. 483–484.
48. Schirmer, pp. 163–164.
49. Richard Taylor, *Index Monasticus* (London: Richard and Arthur Taylor, 1821), p. xx.
50. *Memorials of St. Edmunds Abbey*, ed., Thomas Arnold (London: 1896), III, 245.

51. Gordon Kipling, "The London Pageants for Margaret of Anjou: A Medieval Script Restored," *Medieval English Theatre* 4 (1982): 5–25.
52. Sir William Parker, *The History of Long Melford*, (London: Wyman and Sons, 1873), p. 44.
53. The Rev. Christopher Sansbury, "A Sermon in Stone—and the Great Melfordian Survivors," in *A Sermon in Stone: The 500th Anniversary Book of Long Melford Church* (Lavenham, Suffolk: The Lavenham Press, 1983), p. 52. On John Clopton and the links between Long Melford and Bury abbey see also Gail McMurray Gibson, "Long Melford Church, Suffolk: Some Suggestions for the Study of Visual Artifacts and Medieval Drama," *Research Opportunities in Renaissance Drama* 21 (1978), pp. 103–115.
54. Cora Schofield, *The Life and Reign of Edward the Fourth*, (London: 1923; rpt., Frank Cass, 1967), I, 233.
55. Schirmer, pp. 134, 133, n. 3.
56. Ibid., p. 165.
57. Charles Ross, *Edward IV*, (Berkeley and Los Angeles: University of California Press, 1974), p. 325.
58. Eric N. Simons, *The Reign of Edward IV* (New York: Barnes and Noble, 1966), p. 163.
59. Cf. Mary Clive, *This Sun of York: A Biography of Edward IV* (New York: Alfred A. Knopf, 1974), p. 137.
60. Ross, p. 126.
61. For a detailed account of the turbulent events of 1469–1471, see Ross, pp. 126–177.
62. Clive, *This Sun of York*, p. 184.
63. Macray, Manuscripts of Lincoln, Bury St. Edmunds, p. 139.
64. *Macro Plays*, p. 114 (1. 15).

Is *Wisdom* a "Professional" Play?

DONALD C. BAKER

The title that I have given to my comments is a cheat, for I do not really intend to answer my question. What I do propose to do is re-examine some of our ideas as to what "popular" or "professional" moral drama was—and I do not necessarily equate the terms—in the fifteenth and early sixteenth century. Our *ideas*, I emphasize—not what the drama was, for we can hope for no certainty. And in many respects, *Wisdom*, I believe, is the best of all these plays to help us understand the implications of our own ideas. *Wisdom* is usually spoken of as an anomaly; it worries scholars because it is unlike the other plays. It is "learned," full of Latin, it is stagey; it is, in short, not "popular." It is "different" from the *Castle of Perseverance*, *Mary Magdalen*, *Everyman*, and, above all,

Mankind. Yes, I would say, it is somewhat different; but I would add that *Wisdom* has more in common with the *Castle* and *Mankind* than either of those plays has with *Everyman.* Indeed, it is *Everyman*, usually selected for anthologies as the representative of moral drama, that is the odd man out, the play that is above all concerned with death whereas the others are concerned with life.

It might be objected that I am flogging a dead horse; that the virtues of *Wisdom* and its place in late medieval drama are now much more sympathetically understood than formerly, as witnessed in our present production and in this symposium. Not so. In the most recent survey of the drama, that of the Revels volumes, we find the following, on the whole, thoughtful remarks:

> *Wisdom* is probably the least likely of the fifteenth century moral plays to find favor with a modern audience. It is scrupulously didactic, and seems to be intended for performance indoors to an educated company (perhaps of church dignitaries, undergraduates, lawyers or senior schoolboys) who are accustomed to hearing long discourses punctuated by passages of Latin and will accept a generous helping of pageantry, music and dancing to augment a most meagre allowance of dramatic action.[1]

There is much that is condemning in this passage, but it at least is an improvement upon the kinds of dismissal which the play has received in the past. The passage is, in its copyright, little more than a year old, and is plucked from a volume which, though not intending the kind of coverage provided by Craig's outdated book, certainly intends serious, and, on the whole, sympathetic, coverage for students of a subject to which the writers have devoted many years. If thus treated by its friends, what need *Wisdom* to expect from its enemies? But we are, happily, met in a kind of celebration of *Wisdom*, and I come as an unashamed partisan of the play. I intend to examine the charges against *Wisdom* and compare in each case *Wisdom* to one or more contemporary plays which are admitted by moderns into the canon of the readable, the watchable, the bearable. You, with the experience of watching the play still fresh upon you, will be the judges.

To the charge that *Wisdom* is boring, I can offer no argument. One of the chief weaknesses of critics, I feel, is that so many seem to think that their principal calling is to persuade readers, viewers, and hearers to doubt the evidence of their eyes and ears. No, to those who claim that *Wisdom* is boring, I can only say that I do not share your standards of what is boring.

To the charge that *Wisdom* is stuffed full of Latin, and could, therefore, have been appreciated only by those to whom Latin was a natural tongue of discourse or perhaps an affectation: now, the presence of Latin in a late medieval play is perhaps not terribly surprising. To many even yet, to whom the Latin of the Song of Songs or of the great hymns is not sleep-inducing, it is not unimaginable that Latin phrases and lines from famous hymns and antiphons may well have been powerful and moving, rather than the contrary. And about this Latin I shall have some other things to say in another context. But let us grant that the presence of Latin in a late medieval play is self-condemning; that it is the mark of a playwright who has contempt for his audience on the one hand, or who is attempting to play up to a learned audience on the other. Granted, it is a fault. Then surely the question, on this ground, is merely whether *Wisdom* offends to a greater degree than do those plays which are held up as examples of a greater popular touch, sweeping down the ages even unto our own, glottophobic, times. Let me bore you with statistics. To take only three plays. *The Castle of Perseverance*, much admired, runs to 3,649 lines; among these are, more or less, 85 lines of the offending Latin. I say more or less because a question does arise as to how long a Latin phrase should be before being counted; must it occupy the whole line or just most of it? I have tried to be fair, and in the case of the *Castle*, have counted only those lines totally Latin. I could have run the figure higher had I counted those lines mostly or partly Latin. Now, *Mankind*, the popular and professional of these plays as conceded by everyone, runs to 914 lines (the play was longer, but the manuscript is missing leaves). This popular play has of these 914 lines 28 which are Latin, and I do not, of course, include the "English laten" and the dog-Latin. No, these 28 are genuine Latin, or as near to it as the playwright could approximate, most derived from Biblical sources. The learned and Latinic *Wisdom* runs to 1,163 lines. The number of lines in Latin is 23 *in fine*. There is also relatively little of "dog-Latin," though the play has its fair share of "Englysch Laten." Now it does not require the services of a computer expert to figure out that, roughly, of the three plays *Mankind* has, per line, marginally more Latin than does the *Castle*, and *Wisdom*, least of all.

To continue on this Roman path for a bit longer, we might notice the stage directions. The stage directions of the *Castle* are in Latin except for a handful of musical notations. Except for three, all the stage directions of *Mankind* are in Latin. On the other hand, all but two in *Wisdom* are in English, and one of those Latin directions was added to the manuscript much later. I frankly am at a loss to divine a meaning of these facts—well, not at a loss, exactly, for I have some ideas—but I have no conclusions which might carry much conviction except for one: the generalizations usually made by critics, in passing, about the marked Latinity of *Wisdom* are simply not true, and there's an end on it. I expect that most scholars are misled as to the extent of the Latin in *Wisdom*—this is the charitable conclusion, anyway (i.e., that they are not just repeating one another)—by the fact that there is a certain quality of mind in the play which is not prominent in the others with which I have been comparing it. The Latin, where it does appear, plays an important, thematic and structural role in *Wisdom*; it is used more dramatically, if I may be allowed such a word, in *Wisdom* than in the others, and the impression is created that the Latin lines abound in *Wisdom* whereas they do not. Now, let me be clear, as we say in politics: I am not saying that because *Wisdom* has less Latin than do the other two plays that it is a better play. That fact is irrelevant. I argue only that it is foolish to maintain that *Wisdom* is a dull and learned play, and that one piece of evidence for this is that it is replete with Latin, when in fact it has less Latin than the other plays. It may be a dull and learned play, but the quantity of Latin has nothing to do with it.

Still on the subject of language. *Wisdom* has been accused of being stuffed with "aureate" language. This term generally means polysyllabic Latinate words, frequently original with the author, and implication is that such language is used to disguise paucity of meaning. The word "aureate" is really another word for what Newgyse means when he says that Mercy's body

WISDOM

is full of "Englysch Laten" (1. 124, *Mankind*). Now I do not for a moment deny that *Wisdom* is stuffed with "aureate" language, frequently used for rhyme and so even more conspicuous than if it were hidden within the line. One need look no further than a passage beginning at 1. 446 to discover prominently displayed "replicacyon," "informacyon," "salvacyon," "delectacyon," "generacyon," "pausacyon," "construccyon," "compunccyon," "pollycyon." And one could select similar, equally mind-bending passages. It is no wonder that the late medieval drama provides so many examples for the OED for the first appearance of words. But although the "aureate" words in *Wisdom* may be amusing, where does this lead us? Though "Englysch Laten" is ridiculed in *Mankind*, are we to assume that the playwright avoids it? Nothing, as we say, could be farther from the truth. The author of *Mankind* revels in English laten. Although it is Newgyse who actually uses the term "Englysch Laten" to ridicule a pompous speech by Mercy which rhymes "denomynacyon" and "communycacyon," and granted that Mercy uses a bit more of this polysyllabic stuff than do the three villains Myscheffe, Newgyse and Nought, it is Myscheffe who caps off a passage of polysyllabic nonsense by Mercy with the most marvelous nonsense of all: to Mercy's "serpente," "jugement," "examynacyon," "premedytacyon," Myscheffe adds "calcacyon" and "dalyacyon" and "predycacyon." "Calcacyon," if you could not guess, means not calculation but "trampling," since the figure being used is separating the chaff from the corn. It is true that the "serious" speeches have most of the really paralytic polysyllabic stuff, and that the riotous speeches of the villains and Titivillus have less of it and emphasize disyllabic or monosyllabic rhymes. But this is true of all of this drama, a point that I shall comment upon later. There is less of this business in the *Castle*; reasons are not obvious, but a partial reason might be the somewhat greater age of the *Castle* — there is some evidence that aureate language together with alliteration became more and more popular in the course of the moral drama's history. But there is enough—just no cumulative passages that are fun to cite.

On to other charges against *Wisdom*. A common one is that it is stagey, rather more like the later masque than a lively play like *Mankind*. Another term for this is that there is no action. Now it is rather difficult to define dramatic action. If we look closely at the surviving moral plays, we will find that there is only one—and only a partially moral play at that—*Mary Magdalen*, which has a good deal of action, with the scenes whirring back and forth from Palestine to Marseilles, in the sea and on the desert, Mary being raised by angels with the heavenly chorus looking on. But then, in spite of similarities, *Mary* is treated usually as a saint play rather than as a moral play. What then is the action found in moral plays which *Wisdom* is so prominently lacking? Well, of course, it is difficult to determine from a text exactly what kind and how much of action there was in these plays, except in such cases as *Mary Magdalen* where there is at least a change of scene. Much must have been left to the actors and their *poeta* or producer-director. Just as we can choreograph stage action which may or may not be implied in speech, quite beyond anything that may be called for by a specific direction, so, we must presume, could the companies of professionals or friars, or whatever, of the fifteenth and sixteenth centuries. So a charge of a lack of action must to some extent beg the question. But let us look at plays which are praised by moderns for their action: that must be our test.

Let us take the *Castle of Perseverance* which has in metaphor and actuality an assault upon a castle at its core. As we look about the play we do not in fact notice much action. The play, except for the siege, which is successful, is mostly speeches, as are all the moral plays which, after all, deal with ideas. Death and his dart provide perhaps the most truly dramatic point of the play, not the siege of the castle. Clearly the siege is a siege, and the fighting can go on as long as the director wishes it to; the stage direction uses the adverb "diu." The action is not specified in the directions."Pugnabunt," after all, can cover a multitude of sins. But the famous action could well be dealt with quite quickly, so as to get on with the important matter, the fall of Humanum Genus and his Redemption. The action is spectacular while it lasts. However, consider: all the play leading up to the famous siege is a series of set speeches from scaffolds, solemn processions from one scaffold to another, and solemn conclaves all carried off in a repetitious stanza with a bob-and-wheel at the end. I am not in the business of knocking morality drama, but I find it tiresome that a few are so often praised for what they have not—"liveliness," "realism," "real" speech, etc. In fact, the alleged liveliness and realism are in direct and opprobrious contrast to what the play is about. That it could be fun for the audience, and was intended to be, there can be little doubt; just as there can be little doubt that the business was entirely apart from the essence of the play.

Mankind has been pronounced the most popular of the plays; we may take that word in various senses, for I am sure that all were meant. Though it lacks the banns—the front men who went about in villages describing the play and drumming up business, which the *Castle* has, the play may well have had them, for the first leaves are missing. Most importantly, *Mankind* of all the plays is the frankest about money; the players want it, and in fact threaten to deprive us of seeing Titivillus if we do not cough up. *Mankind* is also the most obscene of the English moral plays. But our theme here is action. What about the action of this play, always praised for its liveliness? In fact, judging from the stage directions, there is next to none. The business consists of Mercy's introductory speech being interrupted by Myscheffe, Newgyse and Nought, and their taunting Mercy. They enter, taunt and leave, enter, taunt and leave; surely this leaves the head less than dizzy with action. By action, scholars have apparently meant the Titivillus business. The "abhomynable presense" of Titivillus is manifested in a way that we can only guess, for the stage directions do not help us. Perhaps the ever-handy firecrackers helped the effect. But to the ACTION which we have all been waiting for. Of what does it consist? It appears that Titivillus can work his devilry by becoming invisible—a pleasant dramatic conventional fiction (it must be, for if we cannot see him, then we will demand our money back). Invisible, he then torments the insufferably complacent Mankind by the ingenious device of planting a wooden board just beneath the surface of the soil so that Mankind cannot plow it. He is also capable, à la Satan and Eve, of communicating in a dream to Mankind that Mercy is in fact an evil wretch, thus causing Mankind to become an apostate. The rest of the play is talk, much of it amusing. But action? Not a lot. To anyone, medieval or modern, who has read Job, the trials of Mankind are not moving. Nor, do I think, are they particularly hilarious. Action is the medium of the miracle play, not the morality. The miracle play instructs by interpretation of events—real events, as far as the audience was concerned. The morality instructs by creating an event around an idea.

But to the ACTION of *Wisdom*. There is not a lot. There are no sieges, no boards in the earth. There *is* a great deal of talk. But surely, the elaborate and vital scenes of Mind, Will and Understanding, each with his followers, dancing, provides as much purely symbolic action as a siege of a castle, as we have seen in the splendid performance and choreography here at Trinity College. The siege and the mime are of the same genre. And there is the opportunity for rather more action than is involved in Mankind's trying to plow through a board. As for earthiness—no pun intended—granted that the rattling obscenities of *Mankind* are not here, but the sophisticated vulgarities of *Wisdom* are more than a match: what other play offers, among other delights, a dancing brothel on the stage, delighting in their calling and hawking their wares? The "sprynge of lecherye" offered us by Will includes in its train Reckleshede and Idleness, Surfeit and Greediness, betrayal of spouse, and "jentyll Fornycacyon," one of those "-yon" words of English laten that the French language has much to answer for.

I do not wish to go overfar in special pleading. But I hope that I have converted some to the idea that the *Castle*, *Mankind*, and *Wisdom* have more in common than not, that they are often praised or condemned for the wrong reasons. I am not arguing that they are essentially the same, though the structures of *Mankind* and *Wisdom* are identical: Before the Fall, the Temptation, Life in Sin (always much the most interesting) and Repentance. But they are of a piece. *Mankind* and

Wisdom follow the same sort of verse-or-stanza form variation, for instance: the serious characters have a straightforward stanza with a progressive pattern of rhymes—in both plays ababbcbc, whereas the villains and fallen heroes speak with a bouncing, in-turning *rime couée*—aaabcccb. The *Castle* is an exception, using the bob-and-wheel (later usually a stanza form associated with villains) throughout. The three share a love of alliteration, which is normally, through far from always, a mark of a fallen character or of a villain. The three plays share a love of fustian—elaborate language saffroned with English laten. They share a fondness for Biblical quotation as might be expected (39 quotes for *Wisdom* versus 26 for *Mankind*; the two are neck-and-neck in their use of popular proverbs: 12 against 13). All three plays have no real setting: we know that *Mankind* is not far from Cambridge, but the scene is the world of allegory; so is that of the *Castle*; so is that of *Wisdom*, though it looks at London and Holborn. All three plays are of East Anglia, and are of that dialect. But they don't "happen" anywhere, as for instance, *Mary Magdalen* does—in too many places, as a matter of fact.

But what is it, really, that disturbs scholars and critics about *Wisdom*? It is not that the play is just dull: it is not, as you have seen this week, except perhaps for the business of the nine points at the end. Besides, no scholar worth his salt would simply say that a play is dull; he feels compelled to say *why* it is dull. But as we have seen, most of the reasons why do not hold water. The fact is that *Wisdom* has a disturbing quality that the *Castle* and *Mankind*, much as I love them, do not, and that is the quality of Mind. It is to this latent intellectual quality that scholars are really referring when they describe the play as learned. They simply mean that the writer has read and thought and that the result is perceivable. More superficially, of course, this quality is apparent in the play's structure. The play is built upon an amalgam of Suso's *The Clock of Eternal Wisdom* and Hilton's *Scale of Perfection*, as W.K. Smart long ago pointed out.[2] But learned lumber in the attic is not what we are talking about. It has a careful differentiation of qualities of the soul that are difficult to dramatize—Mind, Will, and Understanding. It is far more subtle than the usual catalogue of the seven deadly sins, though in fact each sin is neatly attributed to the realm of one or another of the "Mights." Lucifer is a far, far more interesting character, both dramatically and intellectually considered, than the villain of any of the other moralities. He is cunning, evil, logical, reasonable, witty, and also, on reflection, inconsolable that he has lost Heaven. He is a character that analyzes and reflects—really the only one to do so in the moralities. He knows how to attack each of the Mights, quotes scripture to suit his needs, and shows a believable (if anything in a morality is believable) perception of the normal structure of human discourse. He says nothing that cannot be substantiated *per se* in scripture; but he works the argument at a perverse angle. The proper use of the goods of this world; the proper use of power; the proper use of the flesh—all are arguments which any reasonable person would have granted. But then Mind, Will and Understanding yield discretion to the intellectuall symmetry and beauty of argument, of intellectual pride, and ultimately worship themselves—Mind, Will, and Understanding, that is to say, the *act of interpretation* of the letter rather than the spirit. It is the sort of thing that Swift has his characters do in the matter of the Father's boys who run out from Anima's skirts are, of course, the demons of whom Mary Magdalen is delivered ... perhaps one of them is Lucifer's "schrewd boy" whom he had snatched from the audience!

Wisdom is also different from the other moralities in that it alludes to, with clear attitudes, controversies ecclestiastical and legal, of its day—around 1460–80. Other moralities refer to places and persons, but to issues only in a very general way. This is no place to argue the various interpretations of Madame Regent or the Quest of Holborn, but everyone agrees that there are specific references intended.

Having argued for some time the similarities of *Wisdom* and *Mankind* and the *Castle*, I have now emphasized certain differences. But these differences do not, I submit, suggest a difference in genre, or even a difference in audience. Why, then, has scholarship been so keen to find a special audience for the play—the inevitable monastery or school? In large measure because Lucifer tells Will, who is doing divine studies, to leave chastity and take a wife (1. 476). I have no idea why this seems to insist upon a monastery; Will is the student of the three, and the normal, formal condition of the fifteenth century student was one of studying for orders and living nominally in celibacy. I do not insist that the play could not have been or was not played in a monastery; I only insist that *this phrase* does not require it. Scholars have also been keen to assume that *Wisdom*, because of its intellectual nature and careful structure, could not have been intended for the groundlings, as if they could not imagine money being collected after the play from the rude rurals. I can. Whoever played this play were thorough players—the surviving manuscripts are professional in their attention to detail and choreography. We must

Will in the *Tale of a Tub*. It also reminds one of certain critical squabbles of yesterday and today.

But more than this, the play is unique in another sense, in that it is the dramatization of the ancient liturgical quarrel about the meaning of the Song o Songs, the language of which appears in suc prominent passages in the play. The tradition of inte pretation of the *Song* had always split the church, a other case of the letter or the spirit. Each charact particularly Lucifer, has two characters, represent by a difference of color on the inside and outsi "Nigra sum, sed formosa." Love eternal and carnal, spirit and the flesh. The carnal interpretation ta over from the spiritual, as the letter invites one to but, by the intervention of Grace in the form of dom himself, the spiritual interpretation prev Lucifer at the end, for all his wit, his subtlety, i alone with the literal interpretation, with no ho Grace. Though he has lost the case, Lucifer ha retired from the bar.

In this connection I would observe that W has, in mime, what to my mind is the most po scene in the moralities: Anima's appearance, than a fiend" after l. 903. Mind, Will and Unders are invited to look upon Anima, whom we h seen since the beginning of the play. Anima, after all, the whole of which Mind, Will and standing are the parts, has, during their deb acquired on her outside the appearances whi Will and Understanding have on the inside. ognize their true selves under their fancy dr bly disfigured. This image is ancient, but has its power in imaginative literature and dr ages. Perhaps the best known, more moder is Wilde's *Picture of Dorian Grey*. The s not assume that all popular drama for which money was collected, whether acted by seculars or by clerical troupes, confined its subtlety to the shaking of a bladder or the breaking of wind. I see that I still have not defined "professional"; I do not intend to. I say only that *Wisdom* was very probably acted under circumstances and perhaps by the same sort of people as provided the settings and the actors for *Mankind* and the *Castle*. If they were professionals, then likely so were those of *Wisdom*. In fact, if documentary evidence has any bearing on the case, they may well have been the same people and the same places.

The documentary evidence is by no means conclusive, but it is very interesting. Unlike others of the moralities, *Wisdom* exists in more than one copy, one copy and three-quarters, roughly. Both copies are found with collections of other plays, all of those plays having hallmarks which have allowed scholars to describe them as "popular" or professional plays. The full text of *Wisdom*, is, of course, found in the Macro Manuscript, now in the Folger Library, and available to us in a very fine facsimile. It is found smack between the *Castle* and *Mankind*. The provenance of the manuscript is beyond my interest here, but it pretty clearly has its origins in Bury St. Edmunds, in Suffolk, because both *Wisdom* and *Mankind* have the ownership inscription of one Monk Hyngham (Hyngham is simply a local village name, and many monks took their names from their birthplaces, as for example John Lydgate from the village south of Bury in Suffolk). At least three "Monk Hynghams" are known, two of whom were at Bury, one, Richard, abbot at the monastery. Just as importantly, it is called the Macro Manuscript because the Rev. Cox Macro owned it in the eighteenth century; he was a native of Bury. Two other Bury owners' names are associated with both *Wisdom* and *Mankind* in the Macro Manuscript. From these facts one can confidently conclude that 1) both plays, together with the *Castle*, have a long association with Bury, perhaps even originating in the monastery there; 2) though modern scholars insist on describing the two plays as very different kinds of plays, they seem to have attracted the interests if not admiration of the same people. Further, according to Mark Eccles, Norman Davis, and Richard Beadle, *Mankind* and *Wisdom* are in the same hand, except for the last bit of *Mankind*.[3] We would not appear to be dealing with plays that the contemporaries of those plays considered to be totally disparate; they seem to have been tolerated together quite well, however different they may seem to us.

Likewise, the copy of part of *Wisdom* in the Digby manuscript is associated with plays which were pretty evidently travelling plays, professional or popular if you will. It not only appears in the same manuscript with *The Conversion of St. Paul*, *Mary Magdalen*, and *The Killing of the Children*, but the Digby copy is in the hand of the man who copied most of *The Killing of the Children*. To make matters worse, for those who insist upon seeing *Wisdom* as such a very different kind of entertainment, the copy in the Digby manuscript bears the owner's name of Myles Blomefylde, as does also *The Conversion* and *Mary Magdalen*. Myles Blomefylde, though a physician in Chelmsford, Essex in his maturer life, was a proud native of Bury St. Edmunds, a fact which he proclaimed on pages of most of the books which he owned. Clearly, however we may choose to define types of drama, *Wisdom* seems to have been accepted as part of the going dramatic entertainment of the day—existing in two copies, no less! Not a lot can really be deduced from all this, except one conclusion which I do not think any reasonable person can quarrel with: nothing in the documentary history of *Wisdom* suggests that we treat it apart from the other moralities—each of which is, as I have observed, in any case really quite different from the others. Of all the surviving moralities, curiously enough. only *Wisdom* has indisputable evidence that it was acted. There are cuttings in the manuscript. The abreviation "*va va . . . cat*" appears, eliminating the dumb shows of ll. 685–785; this clearly shows that at some point the play was shortened, for reasons at which it is futile to guess. The extremely elaborate stage directions are also quite different from the usual rather brief, even cryptic directions found in the other plays.

On this note, let me attempt to summarize.

All the surviving morality plays are very different from one another, *Everyman* being far more apart from the others than any one of them is from that group. However, they share the love of aureate language, of witty villains, a variation of stanza form befitting the type of character in a scene, an enthusiasm for alliteration, and a fondness for some contact with the audience. But, the *Castle* and *Mankind* are accepted as popular and/or professional plays, whereas *Wisdom* is relegated to the school stage. It may have been. But our knowledge of what constitutes "professional" is none too clear. We think of the collection of money in *Mankind*, or of the banns in the *Castle*. But little or none of what is normally described as the "school" element of *Wisdom* stands up to scrutiny. Its stage directions are in English, not Latin; on examination, its language is no more Latinate or learned than that of the others; it does not have the sustained obscenity of *Mankind* (neither does the *Castle*), but give it credit:

it does have the only mime show of whores in the moralities. It could have been played anywhere, as *Mankind* could have been. Though if it were a touring play, it probably, as would *Mankind* and the *Castle*, have had several set places of playing. In the Macro manuscript containing the whole text of *Wisdom* there is a list of characters, ten in all, representing five speaking parts and five non-speaking. Clearly the Five Wits, for instance, were doubled with the demons, and the characters in the dumb shows, as Merle Fifield has argued.[4] But such a list does not in itself suggest a set place of playing: the cast of characters at the end of the play *The Killing of the Children* has a comment suggesting additional characters, non-speaking, in this case "as many virgins as a man will." There is nothing here that suggests any sort of play generically different from *Mankind* or the *Castle*. Its differences are simply that it has something of the qualities of the later masque, and, most important, that it is far more intelligent than the other plays. We must not confuse this with learning, though the intelligence is based upon learning. It is tightly constructed from a scheme derived from Suso and Hilton and has essentially a single metaphor: the correct reading of the Song of Songs ... a problem that the church has always struggled with.

But *Wisdom* is the only one of these plays that we can say with confidence was indeed acted. The cuttings in the script (present in both surviving mss.) show that at some point the play was shortened, certainly not for reading purposes. The play exists in two copies, unlike any of the others. Both copies exist in collections of plays which bear the marks generally of acted, popular drama; it is copied by scribes who had copied some of the other plays; it bears the marks of ownership of persons who clearly were involved in owning some of the other plays. Now all this, while it is impressive to my mind, need not be taken as proving anything about the contexts in which *Wisdom* was *performed*, though the contexts in which it is *found* are quite indisputably popular or professional contexts. But why, on the other hand, in view of these facts and fairly logical conclusions, should *Wisdom* be *relegated* to a monastic or scholastic setting on the basis of our own quite imperfect ideas of the range and character and quality of the popular or professional drama of the late fifteenth century? We *know* so little. The play was composed by someone of intelligence; it may have been played by a travelling professional group, or a religious, semi-professional troupe; my guess is that it was adaptable for most kinds of playing: the monastic, scholarly setting seen here; a lord's banqueting hall, a school, an innyard, or a village green. The shrewd boy might have been a novice or a village youth. If *King Lear* played in all these settings and to all these people, why not *Wisdom*?

NOTES

1. Marion Jones, "Allegory into Drama: Souls in Jeopardy." in A. C. Cawley, Marion Jones, Peter Mcdonald, and David Mills. *The Revels History of Drama in English*, Vol I: *Medieval Drama* (London: Methuen, 1983), p. 251.
2. W. K. Smart, *Some English and Latin Sources and*

Parallels for the Morality of Wisdom (Menasha, Wis.: George Banta, 1912), pp. 9–25.

3. See Mark Eccles, *The Macro Plays*, Early English Text Society (London: Oxford University Press, 1969), p. xxvii; Norman Davis, review of *The Macro Plays; The Castle of Perseverance, Wisdom, Mankind*. A facsimile edition, David Bevington, ed., *Notes and Queries*, New Series 22, No. 1 (Jan. 1975): 78–79; Richard Beadle, "The Scribal Problem in the Macro Manuscript," *ELN*, XXI, no. 4 (June, 1984): 1–13.

4. Merle Fifield, "The Use of Doubling and Extras in *Wisdom, Ball State University Forum*, v. 1 (Autumn, 1965): 65–68.

Wisdom and the Records: Is There a Moral?

ALEXANDRA F. JOHNSTON

We have just seen, indeed participated in, a performance of the fifteenth century morality play *Wisdom*. This production chose, as its setting, the Abbey of Bury St. Edmunds and, as its occasion, a visit of Edward IV to the Abbey. When I learned from Professor Riggio that this was to be the time and place of the reconstructed performance, the first question that came to mind was the obvious one, "Is such a time and place likely?" The short answer is "I don't know" but, since that would make a very short response to a gracious invitation, let me try, by giving a long answer, to explain why we must, in the end, trust our instincts about the provenance of moral plays since we cannot rely on external evidence.

Last week, *Dramatic Texts and Records of Britain, A Chronological Topography to 1558* compiled by my colleague Professor Ian Lancashire finally arrived from the University of Toronto Press.[1] It is the first fruits of the monograph series Studies in Early English Drama (SEED) set up by the Press to parallel the work of the REED Project. The information contained in Lancashire's work is not complete and will become less so as the evidence being gathered for Records of Early English Drama is edited and published. Nevertheless, the volume is a handy "ready reckoner" to almost all that is currently known about British drama before 1558. If we look up "morality play" in the index and follow the references our problem is clearly highlighted. There is only one piece of external evidence known to concern a morality play. This is a reference from East Retford in Nottinghamshire in a will dated 1499 in which a bequest is made "to a guild of a gilded and jewelled circlet for the image of the Virgin, for a 'ludo de Mankynd, et aliis ludis.'"[2] No other reference survives that is indisputably a reference to a moral play.

In preparation for this paper, I read over the paper I gave in Kalamazoo two years ago about the REED project and records evidence and realized that I barely mentioned morality plays at all. Yet the fifteenth-century moral plays such as those preserved in the Macro text (*Mankind*, *Castle of Perseverance*, and *Wisdom*) had, perhaps, the most influence upon the shape and tone of the drama in the sixteenth century. The form lent itself easily to the possibility of delighting and instructing the young and the powerful alike. It became a central tool in the propaganda wars of the mid-sixteenth century on its way to profoundly shaping the professional theater of the late Renaissance in England. David Bevington's seminal work *From Mankind to Marlowe* pointed out that influence over twenty years ago.[3] Why, then, is there no record of this drama in the external evidence? I suggest that the answer to that question lies in the nature of this drama and in the consequences of that nature.

Moral drama is, more than any other form of early drama, homiletic not to say polemical in its approach. The audience is not being persuaded by the unfolding narrative as they are in the biblical drama or the saints' plays. Nor are they being merely entertained with buffoonery and scatalogical dialogue and action as in the farces. Rather they are being urged to consider choices that arise from questions presented in the context of the drama. They watch the portrayal of the rising and falling fortunes of the protagonist as the vices and virtues—be they theological, political, or social—vie for his soul or his will. The central figure, and thus the audience, is constantly being persuaded by one side or the other through subtle argument, broad comedy, or main force to join them, to change his mind, his religion, his mode of living. The morality form reflects the particular mind and ideals of its author, or, perhaps more correctly, the patron of the play.

Each of the four extant Biblical cycles presents variation in tone and theological perspective as they tell the story of salvation history. However, in this dramatic form, there was a comparatively narrow range within the limits of orthodoxy from which the playwrights could choose their approaches. On the other hand, in the moral drama—particularly the later political moral drama—there was no real limit imposed by theological orthodoxy. Morality drama does not deal with the sacred stories of Christendom; it does not deal with historical figures; it deals with animated abstractions. The figure of "Wisdom who is

Christ" in the play under scrutiny is a theological abstraction; he is not the bleeding sacrifice on the cross.

The morality drama is more cerebral and more abstract than any other dramatic form of the period. The point of view could be chosen quite freely (and at times quite deliberately) by the patron or the playwright to fit the occasion and to make the desired didactic point. Like the later social satires of Ben Jonson and others, therefore, morality drama is by its very nature, ephemeral.

And this, it seems to me, is the very pratical reason why it is not specified in the records. Most evidence from records comes from accounts and, on the whole, accountants were not playmakers. It was their job to keep the books straight and satisfy the auditors. They simply record the receipts and expenditures of the organization for which they work. If the organization was involved in playmaking and lost or made money in the venture, the activity will be recorded, otherwise it will be ignored. There is also far more likelihood that an annual play or one performed frequently will be named in at least some of the records. The cycle play in York is not always named but the abundant evidence of that extraordinary run of close to two hundred years makes it possible to deduce what the play is from a neutral entry. Similarly, the ubiquitous Robin Hood plays that were a standard feature of annual seasonal festivities are easy to identify. Equally easy for the accountants to remember are the names of the saints' plays that gain such attention in the records though not in surviving texts. In all probability those plays portrayed episodes from the life of the local guild or parish patron and would be repeated year after year.

WISDOM

Ephemeral drama like the morality drama performed for a specific purpose at a specific time and place or even a more general one, like the *Castle of Perseverance* that went on tour, is not specifically named in the records simply because it was ephemeral. Accountants give the familiar regular drama names—such as "ludus Sancte Katerina" or "Domesdaye" or "for oure playinge of Robin Hood." I am becoming convinced, however, that such naming is the accident of familiarity, not deliberate intent. Most often references are simply to "our play," "the players," "lusores," "ministralli," "histrioni," "ludus." References to the morality drama lurk behind such general terms. Exactly how we can interpret what the references mean remains a constant challenge to our imaginations.

Let me illustrate this point by references to a set of records I have been working on lately—the accounts and inventories of Eton College. This was a particularly attractive assignment for me because Nicholas Udall was headmaster there from 1534 until either 1541 or 1544 when he left under a cloud and was taken up by the Somersets. Unfortunately (such is the luck of survival) the Eton records are missing from 1534 to 1550! We know Udall was involved in drama there, however, from a single entry in the Privy Purse Accounts of Thomas Cromwell for 1538 where "Woodall the schoolmaster of Eton" is paid the extraordinary sum of £5 "for playing before my Lord."[4] We also have evidence from the accounts and the inventories of the costumes before and after Udall's tenure at Eton. In taking all this evidence together, despite the fact that no plays are named, we can deduce the kind of drama that was being performed in the school in both periods.

The first evidence we have of plays being performed by Eton boys is in 1470–71 when there is a note of several payments to a functionary called John Water "for costumes made in London and for dressing the players."[5] This seems to be the first evidence of traditional performance at Christmas since in 1485 Pennington, probably the schoolmaster, and a painter called Gilbert are paid for providing props for the Christmas play. Nothing more is heard of this play until the accounting system changes in 1525 and suddenly all the expenses for the annual event are listed. In both 1525 and 1526 props are bought "ad duos lusus in aula" at Christmas. The first inventory of costumes comes from 1531 and from it we can begin to deduce what the plays were:

> A cope of tinsel cloth of gold "orfrayd" with red cloth of tissue.
> A coat for our lady of like cloth with St. James shell, pomegranate
> and the griffin in the hem (a marginal note against this entry reads "3 copes made in one for a player and the four remayneth".)
> A habit of scarlet with a hood for the bishop at St. Nicholas' time.
> Another red garment with a hood lined with blue buckram.

It would appear from this evidence that the two plays at Christmas time at least before 1530 were a Boy Bishop/St. Nicholas play and a Nativity Play since a garment for the Virgin is specified. It also seems that the costumes were inadequate since the schoolmaster was paid five shillings for costumes in 1532, and in 1533 some costumes were borrowed from Lord Windsor and others were repaired.

When the accounts resume in the 1550s we have

references to interludes and comedies and, more important, over the decade, expenses for new costumes. The items include coats branched with gold and guarded with leather, skins of gilt leather, coats made of cotton and guarded with cotton of a different color, a fool's coat, pairs of slops and cassocks, kirtles, hats and masks, beards (six of the longest sort and six of the shortest sort), and a gilded mace. It is possible, using one's imagination to interpret the evidence, to deduce that before Udall the boys were performing traditional liturgical plays of the Boy Bishop and the Christmas liturgy as befitted the semi-monastic nature of the foundation. After Udall they seem to be performing humanist interludes. No plays are ever named in the accounts but the evidence can tell us what they were.

Equally creative "guess-work" can be made working from surviving texts. As we all know, most of the texts of early drama have survived without corresponding verifiable local record evidence. These include two biblical cycles—*Towneley* and *N-Town*, two saint's plays—*The Conversion of St. Paul* and *Mary Magdalene*, and the three plays in the Macro text. For all of these texts we are thrown back on the clues provided by the texts themselves (that is, their language and the internal evidence for performance) and on the creative interpretation of evidence from other locations.

For example, two large occasional plays appear in the records of Chelmsford in Essex[6] and of Boxford in Suffolk.[7] These plays were directed by hired "property players" who apparently came to town for a specific purpose and galvanized the townsfolk into a season of excitement. These may be records of the performance of such plays as the *Castle of Perseverance* or *Mary Magdalene*. But I doubt that they are records of the performance of *Wisdom* for reasons I will return to.

In choosing what evidence is relevant to what play we must examine the text itself. *Mary Magdalene* is a wonderful amalgamation of biblical drama, saint's play, and romance. Its form is mixed and, it might be argued, it would have appealed to a mixed audience that could be counted upon gathering in a prosperous market town. Similarly, the *Castle of Perseverance* has a distinctly bourgeois tone to it. If it is possible, and I believe that it is, to make an educated guess about the original audience of a morality from the social status of the protagonist, then the *Castle* must have been directed towards the burghers of a prosperous merchant town. *Humanum genus* is tempted by eminently bourgeois sins, rescued by learned middle-class ladies and ultimately falls because he cannot resist the middle-class sin of greed. I would argue from this and other evidence in the texts of those plays that *Mary Magdalene* and the *Castle* are plays to be performed outside in a civic setting to an audience made up of mixed social standing; but, at least in the case of the *Castle*, the "targetted" audience seems to me to be the upper middle-class.

Mankind, on the other hand, for all its learning, seems to me to be directed to a rural audience. Mankind is a simple farmer beguiled by city-slickers Mischief and the three "N's" who, in the course of the play, get their just desserts, leaving the centre of the stage to the solid local figure of Mercy, the parish priest. By doubling Mercy and Titivillus, *Mankind* can be done with six actors—a troupe small enough to tour. I would argue, therefore, that the *Mankind* text that has survived is a play directed at a largely peasant audience performed anywhere the troupe could gather an audience. I do not believe that the surviving *Mankind* is the one referred to in the East Retford will. And so we come, by a long and circuitous path, back to *Wisdom* and the likelihood of it being performed in Bury for Edward IV.

I said earlier that I do not believe *Wisdom* is a candidate for one of the large open air extravaganzas recorded in Boxford or Chelmsford. Here I entirely agree with Milla Riggio. This is a play designed to be performed indoors quite possibly as we have seen it performed as entertainment for a feast. Because of this, I would argue that this is more of a private than a public play. Its audience is not the generality of middle or lower class East Anglians. As we have seen, Wisdom is portrayed as a king and the sins are the sins of a sophisticated audience. But, and here is the crux of the matter, is the audience predominantly a lay or clerical one?

Professors Riggio and Gibson have presented a persuasive argument that a monastic audience (with a bow to the secular in the presence of the king) was the intended audience of *Wisdom*. Could we shift the focus for a moment? It is true that much of the intellectual thrust of the play is concerned with "authority" but whether this is a secular or religious authority is not made clear. Equally true is that the issue of "maintenance" or the usurpation of the royal prerogative, a decidedly secular issue, is part of the concern. Lucifer does address Mind, Will, and Understanding as "fathers" (1.393), but it is possible such an address could be made equally to serious secular magnates. It is true that Understanding is obsessed with the law and that he frequently cites the sin of simony. It can thus be argued that the playwright is satirizing both the secular courts and the religious courts. Mind falls under the spell of "worldly worschyppe." Although it could be argued that this is more likely to be a temptation more suited to a secular figure, he could be a monk attracted by the secular life. But what about Will? Will's constant theme is sex—and not sex associated merely with animal pleasure. "A woman me semyth a hewynly syght" he says (1.572). His maskers are "six women in sut, thre dysgysde as galontys and thre as matrones, wyth wondyrfull vysures congruent" (at 1.752). Surely these are court ladies and gentlemen. Will does make two references to resort to the "stewes" (ll.749, 800), but it seems to me that his maskers, however lewd their eventual action, start out as courtly dancers. It seems to me that although one can argue that the satire contained in the Will passages was directed particularly at the courtly part of the audience and not at the clerical, it makes equally good sense to argue that the play was commissioned by a great magnate and played in his house to a predominantly courtly audience with some clerics in attendance. I am not here attempting to dissociate the play entirely from Bury. Clearly the connection between Abbot Hengham and the play is very strong. However, we know Lydgate wrote for the court although he was associated with the abbey. I suggest that it is equally possible that this play was commissioned from the abbey by a serious-minded local magnate who was prepared to pay for lavish entertainments. Two possible candidates for such a patron of the arts will make their appearance later in the paper.

But let us turn from the text of the play back to the records. Professors Gibson and Riggio have pleaded an eloquent case in their concern to give *Wisdom* a "local habitation." It is impossible to refute their case absolutely, but let me play the skeptic here.

First of all, we have no direct evidence that this play was ever performed in Bury. Indeed, the only evi-

dence for players that survives from Bury—and this is both the priory and the abbey—is as follows:
1506/7 Account of Prior and Treasurer

> . . .
> Item dat' cuidam Ioculatori   iiij d
> Item dat' ludentibus in Aula & Camera prioris
>   iij s xd

. . .
1530/1 Hostellers' Account

> . . .
> Item datum eodem die (June 23) lusoribus Domini Regis   iiij d
> . . .
> Item datum Lusoribus in aula   ij d
> . . .
> Item datum Herle of darby lusoribus iiij d
> Item datum Lusoribus ducis norfolchi iiij d
> Item datum Lusoribus ducis de Somersett iiij d[8]

Granted this evidence is a whole half century after the proposed performance in the abbey. Granted also that evidence from two isolated years is not conclusive. However, before we conclude that lack of evidence frees us to speculate, let us consider the other external evidence of drama in religious houses.

With the publication of Ian Lancashire's *Chronological Topography* we have at least a short-hand list of the record evidence. The statistics that can be compiled from Professor Lancashire's evidence are suggestive. In all there are ninety-four references from sixty-two abbeys, priories, nunneries and convents. These constitute slightly more than 5 percent of the 1810 references Lancashire lists. Of these, twelve refer to the existence of texts of classical plays, eight are general prohibitions, four refer to liturgical drama (two using boys). There are three references to what seem to be secular plays put on by the school boys attached to Durham, Westminster, and Maxstoke Priory in Warwickshire similar to the plays at Eton. Among some miscellaneous references (which includes some to post-Reformation activity in abbeys in secular hands) is a 1440 censure of a sacrist in Thornton Abbey, Lincolnshire who was lending out vestments to players as well as going about costumed himself and acting before lay folk. Only two references—one from Fountains Abbey in Yorkshire and one from Bicester Abbey in Oxfordshire—might possibly refer to players from the Abbey itself. All other references—twenty-one in all—are references to religious houses that paid travelling or visiting players. These include the references from Bury.

The largest single piece of evidence comes from the account book of the Prior of Worcester Priory, William More. He kept his accounts weekly from 1519 to 1535 and all the references are to visiting companies or patronage given by him to drama and local towns and villages. My colleague Professor David Klausner, who is editing these accounts as part of his REED collection of Herefordshire and Worcestershire, assures me that there is no evidence at all for drama being generated within the priory despite the prior's obvious histrionic interests.

It can be argued that the evidence I have been citing is fragmentary. However it is a sample from all over the country. Furthermore, there is evidence from East Anglia of only visiting players or local secular groups being paid to entertain at the religious houses. At Bungay in Suffolk, for example, there is an early reference from 1407–08 of 6d being given to the "ludentibus de Bungay."[9] This matches evidence from the same period in Berkshire where what appears to be the Robin Hood players from local parishes play for the local corporation or religious house. The account book of Thetford Priory, a Cluniac house not far from Bury, survives virtually complete from 1497–98 to 1540. These are particularly rich, as John Wasson who has edited them for the Malone Society has remarked, but all the references are to players coming to the Priory to perform from the outside. I am afraid that we must face the uncomfortable fact that there is no positive external evidence and more contrary evidence that plays as lavish as *Wisdom* were ever generated from inside a religious house no matter how secular in its outlook.

Let us turn, then, to the alternative that I suggested earlier, that *Wisdom* was commissioned from the abbey by some local magnate. Is there any external support for that hypothesis? In a thesis recently defended at Toronto, Suzanne Westfall has suggested that *Wisdom* is exactly the kind of play one would expect to find produced in a great household. Her reasoning is eminently practical. *Wisdom* demands actors, dancers and other musicians of a professional calibre. Such professionals were just the kind employed by the secular magnates. In her study of the household book of Henry Algernon Percy (1478–1527) fifth Earl of Northumberland, Miss Westfall found evidence that the earl retained three separate groups of servants who, together, could provide the performers for a play such as *Wisdom*. he first group was a troupe of players 4 to 6 in number; the second was the household musicians; and the third was a group of "chapel players," perhaps choir boys retained to provide service music in the private chapel.

The play of *Wisdom* is not simple to produce. I am sure that those involved in the production will be the first to agree. Over the last few decades we have had a lot of experience in Toronto producing medieval and Tudor drama. Yet each production has a special challenge. To produce polished performance takes either hours of trial and error in rehearsal or a seasoned troupe of playmakers who can competently undertake the routine parts of the production and preserve their greater efforts for the special effects. *Wisdom* does not seem to me to be a play for amateurs. If we are right in our mutual conviction that this is, in some sense, a court play, then it would have to be produced up to the standard of performance of the court. The sumptuousness of the costume description argues that it was spectacular. The acting, singing and dancing would have had to be up to the same high standards. This is not a play to be performed by "rude mechanicals" but by seasoned professionals. This consideration reinforces my conviction that *Wisdom* was produced by the paid entertainers of a great magnate.

There is no doubt that many great households retained players and musicians for the very purpose that we have experienced in the production of *Wisdom*. They were to convey to the guests of their master his ideas through the text, his wealth through the sumptuousness of the production, and their skill as performers. After all, when they were not being used by their patron they were touring the countryside. Such command performances were good advertising for their tour. And here, of course, is the flaw in my argument. It is possible that the abbot of Bury himself hired such professionals for just such an occasion as Professor Riggio has conceived. But might I suggest a few possible secular candidates for the original patron of *Wisdom?* The Howards, Dukes of Norfolk, had a seat in this period at Stoke-by-Nayland in Suffolk. Similarly John de la Pole, second Duke of Suffolk, had a household at Wingfield. Despite the merchant origins of the Pole family, John de la Pole married Edward IV's sister Elizabeth. He also managed to survive the Battle of Bosworth Field. I suggest these two names merely as possibilities. I have not done any extensive research on either family but both, later, did have players who went on tour. Norfolk's players, indeed, were paid 4d by Bury St. Edmunds, as we have seen, for a performance in 1530–31.

And so, may I suggest, we have come to a stand-off. We are agreed that this play was intended for a learned and powerful audience of mixed secular and clerical magnates. It is the nature of that mix and the patron of the production that is in dispute. Neither position is unassailable; all evidence is speculative. As I said in the beginning we must trust our instincts when it comes to deciding the origins of the moral plays. My instincts tell me that the patronage was secular and the production professional in every sense.

In Scottish law there is a category of "Not proven." Neither of our cases is proven. May we continue to debate these questions in the hope that from our dialogue will come a truer understanding of the moral plays and their auspices.

NOTES

1. Ian Lancashire, *Dramatic Texts and Records of Britain: A Chronological Topography to 1558* (Toronto: University of Toronto Press, 1984).
2. Ibid., p. 128.
3. David Bevington, *From Mankind to Marlowe* (Chicago: University of Chicago Press, 1962).
4. Lancashire, *Dramatic Texts and Records*, p. 201.
5. All references from the Eton accounts are from the Audit Rolls and Audit Books held by the College.
6. John Coldewey, "Early Essex Drama", Ph.D. diss. (University of Colorado, 1972), p.289.
7. David Galloway and John Wasson, eds. *Records of Plays and Players in Norfolk and Suffolk 1330–1642*, Malone Society Collections XI (Oxford: Oxford University Press: 1980–81), 136–138.
8. Ibid., p. 148.
9. Ibid., p. 140.

INDEX
PLACES, NAMES, TITLES

Aldgate; see London
Arnold, Thomas, ed., *Memorials of St. Edmunds Abbey*, 65n
Arundel, Lord of; see Bury St. Edmunds
Baker, Donald C., 14; "Is *Wisdom* a Professional Play?", 17n, 67; Baker and J. L. Murphy, "The Late Medieval Plays of Ms. Digby 133: Scribes, Dates and Early History," 40, 60nf.; Baker, John L. Murphy, and Louis B. Hall, *The Late Medieval Religious Plays of Bodleian Mss. Digby 133 and E. Museo 160*, 44, 62n, 64n
Baret, John, see Bury St. Edmunds
Bartholomew, A. T. and Cosmo Gordon, "On the Library at King Edward VI School, Bury St. Edmunds," 61n
Beadle, Richard, "The Scribal Problem in the Macro Manuscript," 40, 60n, 86n
Bedericsworth; see Bury St. Edmunds
Benedict, St. *Rule*, 49
Berkshire, 98f.
Bevington, David M., 17n, 43; " 'Blake and wyght, fowll and fayer': Stage Picture in *Wisdom Who is Christ*," 18; *From Mankind to Marlowe*, 37n., 38n, 88, 102n, *The Macro Plays*, 41, 60n, 61n, 66n, 86n; *Tudor Drama and Politics*, 37nf.
"Bevis Marks"; see London
Bible, The: Psalms, 21, 35, Song of Songs, 6, 26f., 30, 69, 79, 84; *The New English Bible, (Song of Songs)*, 37n
Bird, H. Marcus, "The Story of Bury St. Edmunds," in Harry Marsh, ed. *Borough of St. Edmundsbury*, 65n; see Marsh, Harry
Birth of Merlin, The, 38n

INDEX

Blomefylde, Myles; *see* Bury St. Edmunds
Bloomfield, Morton, *The Seven Deadly Sins,* 37n
Bosworth Field, Battle of, 101
Boxford; *see* Suffolk
Bradfield; *see* Norfolk
British Museum, Royal MS 18 D II, 17n
"Bungay, ludentibus de," 98; *see* Suffolk
Bury St. Edmunds, 2, 5ff., 13f., 15f, 17n, 39-60, 60n, 61n, 62n, 63n, 64n, 65n, 66n, 81f., 87, 95-101; abbey church, 46f, 53, 87, 96, 98; abbot, 13, 17n, 40, 48ff., 53, 56, 59, 64n, 100; "Abbot's Cope," 50; Abbot's Great Hall, 3, 7, 15; Abbot Palace, 7, 13, 50ff.,; Account of Prior and Treasurer, 97; Lord of Arundel, 47; John Baret, 49; Bedericsworth, 53; Myles Blomefylde, 41: Richard Cake, 41, 43; John Clopton (of Long Melford), 56, 66n; Corpus Christi Guild, 44f; William Curteys (Abbot), 13, 41, 51, 54f; Earl of Darby, 47; Dusse Guild, 46; St. Edmund 47f., 53, 60; St. James (church), 44f., 51; King's Hall, 51; Liberty of Edmund, 49, 59; Cox Macro, 41f., 81; Thomas Macro, 41f.; Macro family, 61n; St. Mary of the Assumption (church), 51; plays connected with, 43-46; Robert Oliver, 43; Thomas Oliver, 43; Count of Oxford, 47;—Plandon, 43; John Plandon, 61n; St. Robert of Bury, 47; schools of, 42f., 48, 51, 61n; shrine of King Edmund, 57; Jankyn Smith of Bury, 50; Duke of Somerset, 47, 91; town of, 13, 44-53, 59, 62nf., 64n; Weaver's Guild Ordinance, 44; *see* Arnold, Thomas; Bartholomew, A. T.; Bird, H. Marcus; Gibson, Gail McMurray; Gottfried, Robert S.; Hyngham; Lobel, M. D.; London; Lydgate, John; *Macro Manuscript;* Norfolk; Statham, Margaret; Thomson, R. M.; Tymms, Samuel; Whittingham, A. B.
Cake, Edmund; *see* Norfolk
Cake, Richard; *see* Bury St. Edmunds
Cambridge, [University], 51
Canterbury, [Monastery], 48
Castle of Perseverance, The, 8, 16nf., 21, 24, 67f., 70, 73-77, 80-84, 86n, 88, 91, 93f.; *see* Bevington, David; Eccles, Mark; *Macro Manuscript;* Riggio, Milla
Catherine, Mother of Henry VI, 56
Cawley, A. C., Marion Jones, Peter McDonald, and David Mills, *The Revels History of Drama in English,* Vol. I: *Medieval Drama,*

104

INDEX

68, 85n
Chambers, E. K., *The Mediaeval Stage*, 62n
Chasteau d'Amour, Le, 20f.
Chelmsford; *see* Essex
Clive, Mary, *This Sun of York: A Biography of Edward IV,* 66n
Clopton, John; *see* Bury St. Edmunds
Coldeway, John, "Early Essex Drama," 102n
Conversion of St. Paul, The, 82, 93
Cook, G. H., *Letters to Cromwell and Others on the Suppression of the Monasteries,* 65n
Corke, Richard, *see* Norfolk
Craig, [Hardin], [*English Religious Drama of the Middle Ages*],68
Cromwell, Thomas, 91; *see* Cook, G. H.
Curteys, William (Abbot); *see* Bury St. Edmunds
Dahmus, John, "Preaching to the Laity in Fifteenth-Century Germany: Johannes Nider's 'Harps'," 15, 17n
Darby, Lord of; *see* Bury St. Edmunds
Davenport, W. A., *Fifteenth-Century English Drama: The Early Plays and their Literary Relations,* 60n
Davis, Norman, *Non-Cycle Plays and Fragments,* 62n; review of *The Macro Plays,* 86n
Digby Plays, The, 32, 41, 44, 62n, 64n; *see* Baker, Donald C.; Blomefylde, Myles; *Killing of the Children, The; Mary Magdalen; Wisdom*
"Domesdaye" (ludus), 91
Dugdale, Sir William, *Monasticon Anglicanum,* 17n, 65n
Durandus, William of Mende, *Rationale Divinorum Officiorum,* 38n
Durham, 98
East Anglia, 13, 40, 48f., 56, 60n, 77, 95, 98; *see* Bury St. Edmunds, Gibson, Gail McMurray; Norfolk, Suffolk
East Retford; *see* Nottinghamshire
Eccles, Mark, *The Macro Plays,* 16n, 36n, 37n, 43, 61n, 63n, 86n
Edmund, St.; *see* Bury St. Edmunds
Elizabeth, Queen, wife of Edward IV, 2, 10
Elizabeth, sister of Edward IV, 101
Ely, Bishop of, 63nf.
English Kings, 9, 12, 22; Edward I, 49; Edward IV, 2, 9f., 13, 17n, 55-60, 66n, 87, 95, 101; Edward VI, 42; Henry III,

INDEX

51; Henry VI, 2, 13, 17n, 51f., 54ff, 56, 58, 65; Henry VII, "Little Device for the Coronation of," 10, 47; Henry VIII, 44, 47, 53; James I, 53; John, 53; *see* Bartholomew, A. T.; Clive, Mary; Ross, Charles; Schofield, Cora; Simons, Eric

Essex, Chelmsford, 82, 93, 95

Etheldreda, St. ("Sent Audre") 63n

Eton College, 91f., 98, 102n; Gilbert, 92; Pennington, 92; John Water, 92; Lord Windsor, 92; *see* Udall, Nicholas

Everyman, 21, 67f., 83

Fifield, Merle, "The Use of Doubling and Extras in *Wisdom,*" 84, 86n

Galloway, David and John Wasson, *Records of Plays and Players in Norfolk and Suffolk, 1330-1642,* 63n, 102n

Gatch, Milton McG., "Mysticism and Satire in the Morality of *Wisdom,*" 63n

Gibson, Gail McMurray, 5, 13, 39, 95f.; "Bury St. Edmunds, Lydgate, and the N-Town Cycle," 60n, 61n, 62n, 64n; "East Anglian Drama and the Dance of Death: Some Second Thoughts on the 'Dance of Paul's'," 64n; "Long Melford Church, Suffolk: Some Suggestions for the Study of Visual Artifacts and Medieval Drama," 66n; "The Play of Wisdom and the Abbey of St. Edmund," 39

Gilbert; *see* Eton

Gloucester, Humphrey, Duke of, 54

Gordon, Cosmo; *see* Bartholomew, A. T.

Gottfried, Robert S., *Bury St. Edmunds and the Urban Crisis,* 63n, 64n

Hall, Louis B., Jr.; *see* Baker, Donald C.

Happe, Peter, 16n

Hardy, W. K., 50

Henry III, VI, VII, VIII; *see* English Kings

Herbert, William, Lord, and Anne, 17n

Herefordshire, 98

Hill, Eugene, "The Trinitarian Allegory of the Moral Play of *Wisdom,*" 36nf

Hilton, Walter, *The Scale of Perfection,* 6, 15, 18ff., 20, 78, 84 (*Scala Perfectionis*) 36nf.

London, 64n., 92; Aldgate, 49; "Bevis Marks" ("Bury Marks," Bury St. Edmunds' Abbot's Palace), 49, 51; Holborn, 63n, 80; Inns of Court, 63n

INDEX

Long Melford; see Gibson, Gail McMurray; Parker, William; Sansbury, Rev. Christopher; Suffolk

Lydgate, John, 41, 49, 53-56, 60n, 61n, 62n, 64n, 65n, 81, 96; "Ab inimicis, or A Prayer for King, Queen, and People," 56; *Life of St. Edmund*, 54, 56; *Troy Book* 17n; see Gibson, Gail McMurray; Schirmer, Walter

McDonald, Peter; see Cawley, A. C.

Macray, William Dunn, *The Manuscripts of Lincoln, Bury St. Edmunds and Great Grimsby Corporations and of the Deans and Chapters of Worcester and Lichfield, Fourteenth Report, Part 8*, 62n, 63n, 66n

Macro, Cox and Thomas; see Bury St. Edmunds

Macro Manuscript (Macro Plays), 16, 17n, 36n, 37n, 40-44, 47, 57, 59, 60nf., 61n, 64n, 66n, 81, 84, 86n, 88, 93; see Beadle, Richard; Bevington, David; Bury St. Edmunds; *Castle of Perseverance, The;* Davis, Norman; Eccles, Mark; Hengham; *Mankind; Wisdom;* "Wodles, Rainold"

Magna Carta, 53

Malone Society, The, 63n, 99

Mankind, 21, 60n, 67f., 70-77, 80-84, 86n, 88, 94; see Beadle, Richard; Bevington, David; Eccles, Mark; *Macro Manuscript*

"Mankynde, ludo de," 88, 94; see Nottinghamshire

Margaret of Anjou, 55, 58, 65n; see Kipling, Gordon

Marsh, Harry, ed. *Borough of St. Edmundsbury*, 65n; see Bird, H. Marcus

Mary Magdalen, 32, 67, 73, 77, 80, 82, 93f.

Maxstroke Priory; see Warwickshire

Messent, Claude, *The Monastic Remains of Norfolk and Suffolk*, 64n

Mills, David; see Cawley, A. C.

Molloy, John Joseph, *A Theological Interpretation of the Moral Play Wisdom, Who is Christ*, 17n, 29, 37n, 38n

More, William; see Worcester Priory

Mundus et Infans, 8

Murphy, J. L.; see Baker, Donald C.

Nelson, Alan H., *The Medieval English Stage*, 62n

Nicholas, St. ("Sancti Nicholai"), 46, 92

Nider, Johannes; see Dahmus, John

Norfolk, 53, 64n; Bradfield, 43, 62n; Edmund Cake, 43; Richard Corke, 43; Walsingham, 57f.; see Bury St. Edmunds; Messent, Claude; Norwich; Wasson, John

INDEX

Norfolk, Howards, Dukes of, 15, 17n., 47, 49, 100f.; see Suffolk . . . Stroke-by-Nayland
Northumberland, Henry Algernon Percy, Earl of, 99
Norwich, 58, 62n; Bishop of, 13, 17n, 50; Cathedral, 50
Nottinghamshire, 18; East Retford, 88, 94
N-Town Cycle, The, 93; The Passion Play, 32; *see* Gibson, Gail McMurray
Oliver, Robert and Thomas; *see* Bury St. Edmunds
Oxford, [University], 51
Oxford, Count of; *see* Bury St. Edmunds
Oxfordshire, Bichester Abbey, 98
Page, William, ed., *The Victoria History of the County of Suffolk,* 61n
Parker, Sir William, *The History of Long Melford,* 66n
Parry, David, 4
Pennington; *see* Eton
Percy; *see* Northumberland
Plandon,—and John; *see* Bury St. Edmunds
Plautus, 43, 62n
Pole, John de la; *see* Suffolk
Prudentius, *Psychomachia,* 21
Psalms; see *Bible, The*
Rickinghall Fragment, 44
Riggio, Milla, 57, 87, 95f., 100; "The Allegory of Acquisition in *The Castle of Perseverance,*" 17n; "The Staging of *Wisdom,*" 1
Robert, St., *see* Bury St. Edmunds
"Robin of Redesdale," 58
Robin Hood, 90f., 99
Ross, Charles, *Edward IV,* 58, 66n
Sansbury, Rev. Christopher, "A Sermon in Stone: The 500th Anniversary Book of Long Melford Church," 66n
Sarum Missal, 27
Scale of Perfection, The; see Hilton, Walter
Schirmer, Walter, *John Lydgate, A Study in the Culture of the XVth Century,* trans. Ann E. Keep, 65n, 66n
Schofield, Cora, *The Life and Reign of Edward IV,* 66n
Simons, Eric N., *The Reign of Edward IV,* 66n
Smart, Walter Kay, *Some English and Latin Sources and Parallels for the Morality of Wisdom,* 36n, 37n, 38n, 40, 60n, 78, 85nf.

INDEX

Smith, Jankyn; see Bury St. Edmunds
Solomon, "pelles Salamonis," 26
Somerset, Duke of; see Bury St. Edmunds
Song of Songs, The; see *Bible, The*
Sponsus play, 27, 30
Statham, Margaret, "The Guildhall, Bury St. Edmunds," 65n
Sudbury; see Tymms, Samuel
Suffolk, 43, 48, 53, 55f., 61n, 62n, 63n, 64n, 65n, 66n, 81; Boxford, 93, 95; Bungay, 98; John Clopton of, 56; dramatic records, 46; Long Melford, 56, 66n; Lydgate, 81; manor of Rickinghall 44; Stroke-by-Nayland, 101; Thetford Priory, 99; Wingfield, 101; see Gibson, Gail McMurray; Messent, Claude; Page, William; Tymms, Samuel; Wasson, John; Whittingham, A. B.
Suffolk, John de La Pole, Duke of, 17n, 101
Suso, Heinrich, *Orologium Sapientiae*, 5f., 9, 15, 22, 84 (*Clock of Eternal Wisdom*), 78
Swift, [Jonathan], *Tale of a Tub*, 78f.
Tanner, Thomas, Bishop, *Notes of . . .*, 62n
Taylor, Richard, *Index Monasticus*, 65n
Terence, 43, 62n
Tewkesbury, Battle of, 58
Thetford Priory; see Suffolk
Thomson, R. M., "The Library of Bury St. Edmunds Abbey in the Eleventh and Twelfth Centuries," 62n
Towneley Cycle, The, 93
Trinity College, 1, 57, 76
Tymms, Samuel, "Little Haugh Hall, Norton," 61n; *Wills and Inventories from the Registers of the Commissary of Bury St. Edmunds and the Archdeacon of Sudbury*, 61, 64n; *A Handbook of Bury St. Edmunds*, 64n, 65n
Udall, Nicholas ("Woodall"), 91, 93
Young, Karl, "An Interludium for a Gild of Corpus Christi," 62n
van Eyck, [Jan and Herbert], *Ghent Altarpiece*, 22f.
Walsingham; see Norfolk
Warwick, Earl of, 58
Warwickshire, Maxstroke Priory, 98
Wasson, John, 46, 63n, 99, 102n; see Galloway, David
Water, John; see Eton

INDEX

Westfall, Suzanne, 99
Westminster, 98
Whittingham, A. B., *Bury St. Edmunds Abbey, Suffolk*, 65n; "Bury St. Edmunds Abbey: The Plan, Design, and Development of the Church and Monastic Buildings," 65n
Wilde, [Oscar], *Picture of Dorian Grey*, 79
Williams, Arnold, "The English Moral Play before 1500," 37n
Wingfield; *see* Suffolk
Winchester, Cathedral, 16n
Wisdom, 1-16, 16n, 17n, 18-36, 36n, 37n, 40f., 43f., 47f., 57-60, 60n, 63n, 64n, 67-73, 76-85, 86n, 87-90, 93, 95f., 99ff.; *see* Baker, Donald C.; Beadle, Richard; Bevington, David; Eccles, Mark; Digby Plays, The; Fifield, Merle; Gatch, Milton McG.; Gibson, Gail McMurray; Hill, Eugene; Johnston, Alexandra; *Macro Manuscript;* Molloy, John Joseph; Riggio, Milla; Smart, Walter Kay
"Wodles, Rainold," (name in Macro Manuscript), 42
Wölfenbuttel, Codex. Guelf. 78.5, 17n
Worcester Priory, 98; William More of, 98
Worcestershire, 98; *see* Macray, William Dunn
York, [City of], 90
Yorkshire, Fountains Abbey, 98